*What pe_*
DOWNSIZE YOUR LIFE,
UPGRADE YOUR LIFESTYLE

"So many of us (including me!) are drowning in our stuff, and it's not bringing joy or happiness. This is an amazing book on how to downsize and declutter to make room for what matters most. I highly recommend this book, it's life-changing!!"

– Michelle Villalobos, CEO & Founder, The Superstar Activator

"This book cuts straight to the chase on what you need to do to make room for what matters most to you and consciously design a life worth living."

– Tony Jeton Selimi, #1 Bestselling Author of *A Path to Wisdom*, Human Behaviour Specialist and Award Winning Filmmaker

"Rita Wilkins has tapped into the zeitgeist of "third acts" in life. Her advice, personal stories, and top ten tips throughout the book will resonate with anyone, female or male, married or unmarried, who wants to make the most of the last third of their life. She nails the best ways to unlock, unload, and unburden yourself from what you think you can't live without and guides you into a future that you have always dreamed of. Her book is about way more than setting intentions. It is loaded with step by step practical actions to get rid of mental, emotional, and physical stuff. Once done with getting unleashed as Rita has done for herself, she helps you create and explore the best life that works for you. Read this book and bring freedom and adventure back into your life."

–Gerry Lantz, President, Stories That Work

"A must read for anyone, but especially mature purpose-seekers, *Downsize Your Life Upgrade Your Lifestyle* helps you design a life of intention, mission and delight. Rita's insights are one of a kind."

–Angela Heath, Gig Economy Expert

"Rita Wilkins shows us how to live with greater simplicity, generosity and power."

—Steve Harrison, Co-founder National Publicity Summit

"Do you want to kick your clutter to the curb? Do you want to make more room for yourself, your passion, your goals and your joy? Rita Wilkins, in this very transformational book, shows you how to get bigger as your stuff gets smaller. Before you know it — it will be gone and you will appear."

—Dr. Jim Smith Jr., CSP, Best Selling Author of *The No Excuse Guide to Success and From Average to Awesome*, Speaker, Trainer, Coach, Personal Power and Authenticity Expert, CEO Jim Smith Jr. International

"Downsize. Declutter. Design: The 3-D guide for anyone considering a healthy change in lifestyle. Written by Rita Wilkins, a nationally recognized design expert, Downsize Your Life Upgrade Your Lifestyle is the opening salvo to a more fulfilling and meaningful Third Act. Embrace your future now and let Rita's gentle guidance help take you there. It's a 3-D journey you will forever cherish."

— Richard Campbell, Co-Author of *Writing Your Legacy: The Step-by-Step Guide to Crafting Your Life Story*

Simplicity truly increases happiness. Instead, so many people pursue "more stuff" hoping they'll be happier but actually find themselves even less satisfied! This is a must read for anyone who wants a more fulfilling and meaningful life. Downsize Your Life Upgrade Your Lifestyle gets straight to the heart of what you need to do to make the rest of your life the best of your life.

—Jen Groover, Inventor, Author of *What if? & Why Not?*, Global Speaker

DOWNSIZE YOUR LIFE UPGRADE YOUR LIFESTYLE

Secrets to More Time, Money, and Freedom

RITA WILKINS

Published by Kennett & Woods Publishing

ISBN: 978-1-733433-80-8

For more information, visit www.ritawilkins.com

Printed in the United States of America

Dedication

To Mom and Dad,
who taught me to live, love, and lead by example.
Thank you for inspiring me to fly like an eagle.

To Mom and Gene,
who were like parents to me through all the ups and downs of
life. Thank you for loving and supporting me like your own.

To Sean and Kevin,
my sons, the loves of my life.
Who taught me the meaning of unconditional love.
Who taught me to live, laugh and follow my dreams.
Thank you for loving me, believing in me, and allowing us to
learn and grow together.

To Kym and Chethena,
my beautiful daughters-in-law.
Who make my sons light up when you are around.
Who make them laugh out loud. Thank you for traveling
with them as you follow your dreams together.

To my dear friends and family,
who are blessings in my life.
Thank you for your unwavering love and support
as you watched me reinvent myself over and over again.

To my readers,
Thank you for allowing me to use my God-given talents, life experiences, and my voice to make a difference in your life so that you, too, can design and live the life you love each day. Thank you for allowing me to be a part of your journey

BONUS
Quick Start Guide to
Downsizing Your Life,
Upgrading Your Lifestyle

www.RitaWilkins.com

Thank you for buying my book. I am so glad that you have decided to take steps that will help you discover how to design and live a life you love.

This **Quick Start Guide** will make it easier for you to take the information in my book and put it into action so you can actually begin to see results in all areas of your life.

If you want to get started right away…
you can download your BONUS gift at:

Quick Start Guide
to
Downsizing Your Life,
Upgrading Your Lifestyle
at
www.RitaWilkins.com/quickstartguide

Contents

About the Book

This is your year to design and live the life you love

We all want to live a life of purpose and meaning, a life with less stress and more time for what matters to us. But too often life gets in the way. We get stuck. We stop believing it's even possible. Our big dreams and goals get relegated to *someday* or may even be forgotten.

It does not have to be that way!

In this inspiring book, *Downsize Your Life, Upgrade Your Lifestyle,* Rita Wilkins shares how she redesigned her own life, downsizing from a life full of possessions and upgrading to a life filled with passion, purpose and meaning. Her step-by-step blueprint provides tools, tips and strategies that will help you discover how you can be happier and more fulfilled in all areas of your life by living a simpler life with less physical and emotional clutter.

You will learn how to reinvent your own life by discovering:

- What is preventing you from having the life you want now.
- How to let go of your past and get out of your own way.
- How positive and negative mindsets, beliefs and habits impact your personal growth and wellbeing.
- How 5 simple steps can change your thinking and change your life.
- How to reignite your big dreams and believe you can design and live the life you love.

It's time to begin living the life you dream of... why wait? Start now.

THE FIRST ACT

How I Downsized my Life
And Upgraded my Lifestyle

Introduction

"If there is one thing I know for certain, it is that the most important things in life are not things at all. The memories created with those we love, conversations and laughter around the kitchen table, quality time spent with family, friends, and people in need, and a chance to make a difference in the world are the "things" that bring the greatest joy. Choose to live a rich abundant life with less."

–RITA S. WILKINS, "THE DOWNSIZING DESIGNER"

Today, I am beginning yet another new and exciting journey. By writing this book, I hope and pray that I will inspire and empower you to look closely into your own life — to be curious and brutally honest about the quality of life you are actually living. So often we just go through the motions of getting up, going to work, spending a little time with our families, and then doing it all over again the next day. We go through our days without actually thinking about simple changes we could take to make our lives better — much better!

If you are curious about how you could *downsize* areas of your life to *upgrade* the quality of your life, I acknowledge you for taking time to invest in yourself and take actions that will make the rest of your life the best of your life. I will warn you, though, this journey is not for the faint of heart.

It takes real courage to admit that you might be pretending that your life is great when you know it really isn't.

It takes real courage to see that you are using excuses like "too busy" or "not enough time" and admit what you are denying or hiding.

It takes real courage and grit to let go of the fears, guilt, anger, and disappointments that get in the way of being truly free to live the life you love.

If you are using your valuable time to take a serious look at your life right now, this is a wonderful opportunity to get clear about what matters most to you. Once you've gained that clarity, you can use it as your beacon or guiding light to remove things that do not align with your passion, purpose, and "why" from your life.

DESIGN THE LIFE YOU LOVE

Best of all, this is the opportunity of a lifetime to design the life you love; one that will give you more time, money, and freedom to pursue what matters most to you. Your words create your world. Why not create a life—your life—that you can hardly wait to wake up to each morning?

If you could live an abundant life with "less" so you could live more, why wouldn't you?

Think about it.

What would it be like to live a life with less stress, less overwhelm, less scarcity, and have a life with more energy, more excitement, and endless abundance?

It is not too late to have the life you dream of, the one you may not even think is possible. It won't happen overnight, but you could start by taking baby steps right now.

Change is never easy, but if you want to live a life you love, isn't it worth investing time and effort to have what you really want and say "yes" to life—your life?

As I sit here in my tiny "jewel box" apartment in the beautiful historic area of Philadelphia, even though I gave away 95% of my possessions and I am now living with 5% of what I once owned, I have all I want and all I need—and I've never been happier. Content. Fulfilled. Excited about life. Reinventing. Listening. Anxiously anticipating "what's next!"

That's why I am so passionate about this subject and why I decided to write this book and share my own personal downsizing journey. My goal is to inspire you to take a close look at your life and find a way to make it more meaningful, more rewarding and more joyful.

CHAPTER ONE

My Journey to Living Abundantly with 95% Less

"The day she let go of the things that were weighing her down was the day she began to shine the brightest."

- Katrina Mayer, Success.com

I had hoped to begin a wonderful new life in 2007. Instead, it was the beginning of one of the most challenging and difficult times of my life.

As a single mom, nothing mattered more to me than "my boys." I did everything I could to ensure that, despite my divorce, my two sons would thrive and grow into happy, healthy adults who would meet and marry amazing women. That's exactly what happened. Nothing makes me happier than to know they are happy, loving and loved.

While I look back on that time of my life as one of the most difficult times, it was also one of the best times of my life. My sons were successfully launched. I was so proud of them for who they had become and for having such promising lives ahead of them.

That would have been my story too, but it wasn't. In 2007, I married a man I should never have married. My mistake, but also, my dream of a happily-ever-after life was dashed. We had built a big, beautiful house that would have been our "dream home". After the divorce, my "dream house" actually became a nightmare. I was overwhelmed by the amount of time and effort it took to care for a large house and property by myself. I had so little time to actually enjoy it with family and friends and was anxious about the amount of money I was spending to maintain it.

I had no time, no money and no freedom to enjoy life.

I also owned a large condo, which housed my successful interior design firm. It served as an impressive, dynamic space for my team of designers and staff to design and implement thousands of incredible interiors all over the country. During those 25 years, we experienced considerable financial success. We weathered several economic downturns and always managed to reinvent ourselves to adapt to the changing marketplace. I actually enjoyed those challenges to not only survive but to thrive during difficult times. This turned out to be one of my greatest strengths, which I had numerous opportunities to exercise again and again.

But this time, it was different. I was different. Something had shifted in me, but I was not sure what it was. The overhead of the office building, my business, house, and failed marriage were all starting to bear down on me. My life was spiraling out of control and I saw no immediate way out. Frankly, I was afraid, but told no one, not even my boys or family. I told myself I was strong and resilient, that I had been through a number of difficult times before and that I would discover new ways to reinvent both my personal and professional life again.

The timing could not have been better for what happened next. My son, Kevin, who was serving in the Peace Corp in Senegal invited me to visit him. There was nothing I needed more than to spend quality time with my son, whom I hadn't seen in over a year and to experience the life he was living in his tiny village 8,000 miles from home. That trip enabled me to get away from the stresses of the house, business, the building, and regret over my toxic marriage. It offered me time to clear my head and get perspective of my own life—and if I were leaving, I hoped to find clarity and direction for my next chapter.

LIFE-CHANGING MOMENTS

That trip to Senegal changed my life. As I shared in my TEDx Talk, "Downsize Your Life: Why Less is More," traveling to my son's village was the trek of my lifetime to date. For twenty-four hours, we traveled in buses with holes on the floor, cars with no working gauges, and the back of pickup trucks. The travel itself was an unforgettable adventure, but what I experienced with the villagers was what turned my life around and allowed me to see my life through a whole new lens.

Within minutes of arriving in my son's remote little village, the village elder presented me with a live scrawny chicken, a gift I knew in my head and my heart was of extreme value. That evening, Kevin's African mother prepared a delicious dinner for 15 people that included that little chicken. During the day, she had also carved a wooden spoon for me since she understood that I may not yet be accustomed to eating with my hands. As she served the food, she pushed the better parts of that small chicken toward my son and me. In that moment, I realized these villagers had almost nothing, yet they were joyful! I wanted that!

A month later, as I boarded the plane to return to the United States, I will never forget my son's loving words of wisdom,

"Mom, I haven't seen you this happy in quite a while. You can have a simpler life if you want it. Think about it."

I arrived home to my big, beautiful home and as I walked through each area, room by room, all I could see was my world of excess. Clearly, something had rocked my world as I kept hearing my son's words and remembering the villagers. They had almost nothing but they were happy. On the surface, it appeared that I "had it all," but all I could see now was "stuff"—and way too much of it!

A second life-changing moment occurred when my older son, Sean, who lived in San Francisco, called me at work to announce he was going on a six-month sabbatical to South America to "get clear on what direction he wanted to take in his career." He assured me that he had saved plenty of money and that I should not worry. I remember thinking "Sabbatical! You are thirty years old for God's sake!" I was certainly happy for him and proud of him for taking time to assess his life and career, but as I looked around at my beautiful office building and all of the expenses and responsibilities associated with it, I couldn't help but realize how trapped I was with no easy way out.

Prior to departing for South America, Sean flew into Philadelphia to say goodbye. At dinner that evening, he handed me Tim Ferris's book, *The Four-Hour Work Week*. While grateful for the book, I remember thinking, "There is no way I could do that!" As he prepared to board his flight for his six-month sabbatical, I will never forget his loving, wise words, "Mom, you can have a better work life balance too if you want it. Read the book!" I went home and read the book over the weekend.

When I returned to work on Monday and as I turned the key to the same door I had been opening for twenty five years,

I suddenly realized, "I do not want to do this anymore!" I did not want all of the burden and expense of owning the building. I wanted to start lightening my load, to downsize my space and responsibilities, and to be less encumbered. After all, I knew in my head and my heart that the building did not define who I was as a woman, a business person, or a mom. A few months later, my office building was sold.

GETTING UNSTUCK

But I continued to remain stuck in my big, beautiful home. Looking back, I realized I resisted letting go of my dream home where I lived there alone. It took 3 years for me to admit that my house had become a symbol of my success after many years of hard work. The journey to letting go of my home would take time. Even as my life continued to spiral out of control, I proceeded to add to my collections of beautiful, meaningless stuff. I shopped for even more clothes, more shoes, and more handbags trying to grab onto meaning.

Then, in December 2015, at a Christmas party in my home, a friend asked me, "Rita, how much longer are you going to live in this big house by yourself?" I remember saying, "In one year I will be living in a tiny apartment in Philadelphia." I have no idea where those words came from, but in January 2016, I sat in the middle of my living room floor, looked up, and cried. I had no idea where to begin, but my journey to downsizing my home and living with less began.

That yearlong journey was one of the most challenging, most revealing and most rewarding years of my life. During the process of decluttering and downsizing my home, I discovered the real me that was hiding underneath all of that beautiful stuff.

A YEAR OF LEARNING TO LET GO

Downsizing is a rollercoaster of emotions:

- The thrill and excitement of a vision for a new lifestyle.
- The unsettling and confusing decision fatigue.
- The dream and promise of a simpler life with less.
- The daily struggle and exhaustion of letting go of years of excess accumulation.

I spent an entire year of my life downsizing my big house. To say it was easy would be a lie. I was confronted daily with:

- One more drawer or cabinet that was crammed with things I didn't even recall buying.
- One more useless gadget I thought would make life easier.
- One more closet filled with clothes that no longer fit or that I hadn't worn in years.

Although I was embarrassed, ashamed, and guilty about the excess and overspending, I continued to buy more.

At the end of the day, I was physically exhausted and emotionally drained… and so alone. At first, I tried to tackle this downsizing project on my own, thinking I could chip away at this overwhelming task day by day in my spare time. After a month into my solo attempt to be superwoman, I picked up the phone to call my family and friends to say "Help!"

Those calls generated one of my first big discoveries: I didn't have to do this alone. I realized the importance of having a team to accomplish such a big undertaking. It was at that point that I decided to create a team and schedule one or two of them to meet with me for 4 hours on a Saturday or Sunday so I would garner the physical and emotional support required to downsize my life. Ultimately, I gave away 95% of what I once owned to people who needed or wanted it.

CONFRONTED BY CLOTHES

It was a dreary winter day. Perfect for attacking the first of my many closets… or so I thought. I opened the door to one of my master bedroom closets and stared at a room full of clothes filled with beautiful dresses and suits, many of which had not been worn in years. Some still had tags on them.

Touching each piece of clothing, I was filled with emotions ranging from guilt to shame to disgust. What made me purchase so recklessly? Did I really need all of these? Weekend after weekend, I would fill my lonely days in search of "the perfect little black dress and shoes" for the someday perfect date. Then I counted four other little black dresses that looked just like the other ones.

Among all of the clothes, a particular marine blue suit captured my attention. It was the suit that I wore to the White House for Kevin's exit interview with the President. For two years after college, he worked in the Bush White House in the office of Presidential Personnel. Upon leaving his position at the White House, it was customary for the immediate family to be invited into the Oval Office to meet the President. That one piece of clothing helped me recall a very proud "mommy moment." Never wanting to let go of the memories, I struggled to let go of the clothing that reminded me of special times in my life. But why? They were just clothes… and way too many of them.

As I stood there in the middle of the large walk-in closet surrounded on three sides by clothes I mostly no longer needed or wanted, I began to envision women who would be thrilled to have even one of these beautiful suits or dresses.

What was I waiting for? The new simpler life that I said I wanted did not have room for this kind of excess. My vision for that simple life with less was the motivation that I needed.

I first removed all the clothes I hadn't worn in at least a year. Next, I tried on those that I wanted to keep. If they didn't fit me when I tried them on, I put them in the donate pile. The clothes that remained hanging were still too many, but I realized I could do a second and, perhaps, a third edit on another day.

Next, I folded the "donate" clothes into neat piles and then put them into boxes. I immediately loaded the boxes into my car so I wouldn't have second thoughts.

As I pulled out of my driveway and started to drive to my favorite women's shelter, it started to snow. Big, fluffy snowflakes. I rang the bell to the shelter and told the woman who answered the door that I had women's clothing to drop off. Within minutes, I was warmly greeted by three women who helped me unload the boxes from my car. I wasn't expecting their assistance, but it was definitely appreciated.

I knew that this particular shelter welcomed donations of professional women's clothing so their residents could wear them to job interviews. One of the women said that she could hardly wait to get a good job so that she could get a nice apartment for herself and her children. I felt a warm glow knowing that I was doing the right thing. This was just one woman of many who would benefit from the clothes that had been hanging uselessly in my closet.

Driving home, I was overcome with gratitude. I realized that there was so much more that I could do and must do. By letting go of my excess stuff, I was gaining so much more in return.

As I walked into my home, I suddenly felt lighter. I also realized I didn't always have to be strong and I didn't have to do everything by myself. There were people in my life who cared for me and told me they were willing to help. I was finally willing to accept their assistance.

For years as a single mother, I didn't allow myself to be vulnerable or ask for help. The process of cleaning out my first closet helped me to see my life through a new lens. I began to pick up the phone more often to ask my friends and family for help.

In retrospect, I would take this exact same journey all over again. Downsizing my life has given me the simple joy-filled life that I experienced in Senegal. I now have all I want and all I need, and I've never been happier. As "The Downsizing Designer," I am committed to sharing my downsizing journey so that I might inspire others to consider living a simpler life with less.

Top 10 Lessons I Learned from Downsizing My Life

1. I learned to grieve and let go of my past disappointments, failures, and resentments so I could move forward.

2. I learned a new definition of success.

3. I learned how to stop making stuff mean something.

4. I gained clarity about what matters most to me and why.

5. I realized that owning so much stuff detracted from my happiness, contentment and peace of mind.

6. I learned to love myself for all I am and all I am not.

7. I learned to stop comparing myself to others. I realized that I have enough and I am enough.

8. I let go of having to be perfect.

9. I gave myself permission to be open, vulnerable, and authentic.

10. I realized how much richer my life is even though I own so much less.

CHAPTER TWO

The Impact of Living With Less

"Anything in life worth having is worth working for."

—ANDREW CARNEGIE

Soon after moving to my tiny apartment in 2016, *Delaware Today Magazine* asked if they could send a reporter and camera crew to interview me about downsizing from my 5,000-square-foot home in Chester County, Pennsylvania to my 867-square-foot apartment in historic Philadelphia.

Over the past thirty-five years, *Delaware Today* had featured many of our interior design projects in their magazine, including my large home, so their readers had a natural curiosity about why I would do such a thing and what it was like to have made such a drastic change in my lifestyle. After all, wasn't an interior designer supposed to live in a big, beautiful home? In her article, Eileen Smith Dallabrida captured the true essence of my tiny living and city life. She conveyed the simplicity, the freedom, and my joy of living with less—95% less.

Within weeks of appearing in the magazine, I started to become known as "The Downsizing Designer," a moniker I now welcome and embrace. If my downsizing journey inspires others to live a simpler, more meaningful life, then I gladly accept being the poster child for joyfully living with less. It gives me great pleasure to know that I have the opportunity to impact many lives by speaking to audiences all over the country and sharing my story.

Now that I have downsized my life, I have more time, money, and freedom to use my voice and platform as "The Downsizing Designer" to change lives. This new effort has grown into my passion - sharing the benefits of living with less so you can live more, love more, matter more. Most importantly, it is achievable for anyone who wants it. If I can do it, so can you!

I must admit, however, that the idea of living a simpler life with less did not always have the same appeal to me that it does today. The reality is, if I had known then what I know now, I would not have scaled up as much as I did, nor would I have accumulated so many belongings. Note to my younger self: own less stuff.

BIGGER, BETTER, MORE

As one of the 76 million people in the baby boomer generation, I bought into the mass marketing messages that encouraged us to believe that a fancy new car, an even bigger house, and designer clothing are what we need to be happy. My generation, born between 1946 and 1964 helped shape the world of consumption of bigger, better, more. Baby boomers have more disposable income than any previous generation, so we created a movement that encouraged the acquisition of goods and services in ever-increasing amounts.

When it came to the ultimate symbols of success and status, the lines between happiness and what really mattered became blurred. The more you bought, the happier you would be, or so the marketers would have you believe. Eventually, many baby boomers came to define themselves and their meaning with name brands, dollars in the bank, the number of cars and possessions they owned, and the expensive vacations they took each year. This was my story and my life. Looking back, that lifestyle was crazy, empty, and meaningless. I felt trapped and saw no way out. What I did discover, though, was that one more pair of beautiful shoes only brought buyer's remorse—not the happiness and simple life that I most wanted and secretly yearned for.

While I am not proud of that overindulgent chapter of my life, the reason I share my story is because it also to be the story of many other baby boomers. If this describes your life, I'd like to suggest that you consider disrupting that unending cycle of mindless consumption and experiment with living with less. When you do, you're likely to find that you will have more time, money, and freedom to pursue what really makes you happy, and you will gain a far deeper sense of satisfaction, meaning, and fulfillment.

I have become a strong advocate and spokesperson for living a simpler, more meaningful life with less because I have personally experienced the impact of doing so. Living with less has changed my life. In addition to being happier and more content, I was surprised to discover that I became much more effective and productive in business and in life. So, whether that means reducing the stuff that weighs you down or eliminating anything that is not important or essential, these changes will allow you to intentionally focus all of your energy on ONLY the things that are MOST important to you.

INSPIRATIONS TO LIVE WITH LESS

In his inspiring book, *The Power of Less*, Leo Babauta encourages readers to look at each area of their life to discern what consumes too much of their time, money, and energy. He defines it as "the fine art of limiting yourself to the bare essentials in business and life."

Leo Babauta's shared six Power of Less principles, which I have found valuable:

1. Set limitations.
2. Choose the essentials.
3. Simplify (eliminate the non-essentials).
4. Focus (a tool for becoming more effective).
5. Create new habits (for long-lasting improvement).
6. Start small (to ensure long-term success).

Learning how to intentionally focus on less can transform your life. It reduces stress and overwhelm. Your life becomes simpler, more manageable, and that helps you stay focused on what is most important to you. I keep this list of principles as a constant reminder of why I started my downsizing journey in the first place.

Perhaps, one of the greatest influences on my desire to own less is Joshua Becker, the founder and editor of the Becoming Minimalist website. He is one of America's leading voices for the minimalist movement. I remember the exact moment I first read Joshua's emotional story that inspired his decision to live with less.

One beautiful day, as he cleaned and organized his garage, his young son kept asking him to play, but Joshua's response was, "When I'm finished cleaning the garage." At the end of the day, he asked himself, "What could be more important than spending time with my son?" In that moment, he realized he had allowed his stuff to overtake his life and he needed and wanted to own less.

That story touched my heart and made me cry, longing to recapture some of those moments where I was too busy managing my stuff to spend more time playing with my own two sons. While my boys are now happy, healthy adults, I still feel a pang of regret about the times that I could have spent with them rather than organizing my ever-growing piles of stuff. Joshua refers to it as "finding the life you want under everything you own."

His book, *The More of Less* inspired me to take action so I could make more room in my life for what I really wanted. While the downsizing journey is not an easy one, the lasting impact is profound. As with everything else in life, if it is worth having, it takes work, commitment, and tenacity.

Downsizing has changed my life and it can change yours too if you want it badly enough. It requires relentless commitment to your vision, especially when you feel like giving up. The reality is, the journey just keeps unfolding. I am still confronted daily with "clutter creep" because when living in a tiny space, even the smallest of items like mail, magazines, and shoes are more visible and distracting than in a larger home. But because of my commitment to a clutter-free environment, it is worth the effort for me to consistently put things where they belong. This is such a small price to pay for the peace of mind of living with less.

Life Changing Benefits of Living a Simpler Life with Less

TIME
- ♦ More time to pursue what matters most.
- ♦ Better work-life balance. Work less, play more.
- ♦ The opportunity to give back, to be of service to others in need, and make a difference.
- ♦ More "you" time. Time for personal and professional growth.
- ♦ Extra time to listen and engage with others to create better relationships.

MONEY
- ♦ More money. Less spending, less debt, less stress.
- ♦ New habits and discipline to accomplish financial goals and increase productivity.
- ♦ Less waste, less consumption, and more responsible use of resources.
- ♦ More gratitude for what you have. Less interest in needing or wanting more.
- ♦ More mindful spending on experiences rather than stuff.

FREEDOM
- ♦ Less meaningless stuff makes room for more meaningful experiences.
- ♦ More freedom to pursue dreams and to discover new passions.
- ♦ More opportunities to reinvent and design the life you love.
- ♦ Less fear of failure, more resilience to bounce back and learn from setbacks.
- ♦ Less mental clutter. More peace of mind and happiness.

CHAPTER THREE

Lifestyle Design—What Is It?

"Create the life you can't wait to wake up to."

—JOSIE SPINARDI

INTERIOR DESIGN

What is it?
A creative process that uses abstract ideas to solve problems and create unique solutions for each clients' wants, needs and wish list for residential and commercial interiors.

Innovative design concepts that enhance and impact the beauty, comfort and efficiency of how we experience the environment we live, work and play in.

Interior Design Services Design Tools

- Design Concepts
- Space Planning
- Design Development
- Design Consultation
- CAD Drawings
- 3D Renderings
- Blueprints
- Project Management

LIFESTYLE DESIGN

What is it?
Living the life you love… by design.

Living in alignment with your values, passion and purpose each day of your life.

Intentionally choosing how to spend your time, money and energy to create and to experience a higher quality of life in all areas of your life.

Lifestyle Design Services Design Tools

• Journaling	• Breakdown barriers
• Inventory your life	• Downsize/ Declutter
• Assessment	• Prototyping
• Visualization	• Action Steps

LIFE IS A PICNIC

As the daughter of an Air Force pilot, our family had many opportunities to live in various parts of the world. One of my favorite locations was Hahn Airbase, Germany where we lived for almost 5 years. While living in Germany, our family of seven took frequent road trips to neighboring countries. Our mom usually instigated these adventures, and Dad was the consummate planner. In so many ways, they were the perfect team. She was curious, a lifelong learner, and creative visionary. He was our rock, with the open mind and a steady temperament that served him well as he engaged in and followed through on her ideas and inspirations.

Her passion for travel, meeting new people, experiencing different cultures and seeing the beauty in all of it was what she wanted most for our family. Long before "lifestyle design" became part of my vocabulary, Mom designed a lifestyle for our family filled with experiences and memories that have lasted a lifetime. Their gift of experiences surpasses any wrapped presents I received for Christmas or birthdays. The memories of our times together as a family became part of the fabric of who I am and, without a doubt, influenced my passion for living each day to the fullest.

One of my most cherished childhood trips was a picnic in the foothills of the Swiss Alps. What makes that trip so memorable is the stark contrast between the breathtaking beauty of the snowcapped Alps and the absolute simplicity of our picnic lunch of peanut butter and jelly sandwiches. Even as a child, I somehow realized we could have been anywhere in the world as long as we were experiencing those events together as a family. It just so happened that mom chose the Alps for this particular outing. As Dad maneuvered our large black and white 1960 Oldsmobile up the narrow roads and around the tight switchback turns, each new vista was even more spectacular than the previous one. We each vied to be the one who would discover the perfect spot for our gourmet lunch.

Just as we rounded one of those bends, my entire family collectively shouted, "That's it!" Dad pulled over to a safe spot next to an alpine trail that was covered with the most beautiful array of bright jewel-colored wild flowers that I had never seen. We were surrounded by nature's delicate balance of red, yellow, pink and purple blossoms in full summer bloom. Just as Mom laid out our big, well-used picnic blanket, a large brown cow with eyes as big as golf balls meandered toward us, seeming to enjoy the company.

While we were frightened at first, we realized she was just being curious. After all, we were the intruders in her little piece of heaven. We sat down to savor our homemade lunch against the backdrop of a deep blue sky, the majestic mountain peaks, the clanging of the cowbell and the scent of alpine flowers. What do I remember most about that day? The smiles, the laughter, the love and how much I still love PB and J sandwiches!

Each time I share this story and many others like it, I can't help but be amazed at how our mom **intentionally created moments and experiences** our family will remember for our lifetimes. She was the first (and the best) lifestyle designer I have ever known!

WHAT IS LIFESTYLE DESIGN?

The story I just shared with you is the essence of lifestyle design. I define lifestyle design as **living life on purpose in all areas of your life**, including relationships, family, work, health, finances, and spirituality. It is how you experience your own life. It is how you show up each day living in alignment with what matters most to you so you can live a higher quality of life.

Lifestyle design is about choosing to be present in each moment so you can capture the beauty, the sights, the sounds, the smells, the laughter, and the love. It is intentionally creating and embracing experiences that change you, mold you, and influence you.

As you consider what lifestyle design means to you, give some thought to these questions:

+ Have you designed your life the way you want it to be or are you stuck in a mediocre lifestyle and routine that no longer serves you?
+ Are you living life each day as if it were your last?

Lifestyle Design involves making choices about how you use your time, money, and energy, as well as your God-given gifts so you can live the life you love... by design. It is living with intention and on purpose.

Being mindful of even the smallest decisions you make each day can make the biggest difference, not just in your own life but in the lives of those you love. Here are three examples of the powerful impact of small choices:

- Jason, a busy young executive, committed to leaving work early so he could watch his son's ball games through his Little League years and all the way through high school. Rearranging his work schedule was a small price to pay for the loving relationship Jason has with his son many years later.

- As a single mom, Miriam juggled many roles but she was committed to creating a loving, stable, and nurturing home for her three children. She made dinner time together her highest priority. Today, her teenage kids love bringing their friends over to hang out at the kitchen table… music to every mother's ears.

- Karen is a retired grandmother who offered to spend at least 2 days a week taking care of her grandchildren while her daughters were at work. These two years of precious moments with her grandchildren were priceless, not just for Karen but for her entire family.

Choices made. Lives changed. All based on personal values and what mattered most to them. They each chose to be present to what was happening in their lives at that time. They realized that the choices they made today would impact their tomorrows. They understood that they would never get those moments, days and years back. They intentionally prioritized how to use their time, money and energy to impact the quality of their lives and the lives of those they loved.

"Shoulds" and "Have-tos"

Sadly, many people live their lives as if they were programmed to do or to become what others want or expect them to do or to become. Living in the shadow of "shoulds" or "have-tos" means they are not living a life of their own choosing.

Several years ago, I mentored a young woman who had checked all the right boxes. She went to a prestigious college, graduated summa cum laude, and was accepted into one of the finest law schools in the country. An overachiever, she persevered through many grueling years of hard work, then landed a position at one of the largest law firms in the area.

However, when I first met Cindy at a networking event, she was miserable. After several conversations, she admitted that who she had become and all that she had accomplished did not reflect her own true passion. She had been living a life her parents wanted for her. She was unhappy, unfulfilled, and yearning for something that aligned more with her desire to empower other women to live their dreams.

Her parents might have had good intentions in encouraging her to aim for these lofty goals, but Cindy never learned to make her own decisions and did not trust herself to make choices that reflected her own wants, needs, and wishes. She had been so programmed to have the big life decisions made for her, she was startled and speechless when I asked her what was stopping her from pursuing her own dreams. It took several years and a tremendous amount of courage for her to walk away from her parents' idea of a successful career.

She realized that in order to have the life she really wanted, she had to redefine her idea of success. It wasn't easy and it didn't happen overnight. But when she finally faced her fears and insecurities and started to visualize her unique dreams, she was able to achieve what she most wanted. Today, she is the executive director of a non-profit, a position that is fulfilling and meaningful to her. She is grateful to have the opportunity to empower other women to make decisions about the direction of their own lives. Ironically, her non-profit helps women find employment that contributes to their personal, professional, and financial growth so they can realize their own dreams.

Cindy disrupted the trajectory of her own life by challenging herself to question what mattered most to her. She chose a career path that aligned with her true passion, one that is rewarding and making a difference. This is just one example of how life-altering lifestyle design can be. It changed her life; now she is changing the lives of others.

According to *Success Magazine*, "Over 50% of Americans are unhappy in their jobs and over 50% of America's marriages end in divorce." Not great news. Certainly not a way to live—really live.

When do you know that you are not living the life you are meant to live?

Do you often find yourself thinking these thoughts?

+ You would rather be anywhere other than here. You have a feeling that just about anything would be better than... You fill in the blank.

+ You want so much more, but you may not know what "it" is you are missing.

+ You have a dream and this is not it. Your dream is so different from the way you are living now that you can't imagine how you could achieve it. So you just don't try.

Perhaps, like Cindy...

+ You feel trapped, afraid, and see no way out of your current circumstances.

+ You feel stuck in a career that provides a paycheck but no meaning or fulfillment.

- You are in a toxic relationship that continues to drain life and energy from you.
- Your life is a vicious cycle of pressure and demands that leave no time for you and your own personal and professional development and growth.

While living the life you love might seem like a distant dream and impossible to achieve, I would like to challenge your thinking.

DON'T LET FAILURE STOP YOU

One of my favorite sayings is, "If it is to be, it is up to me." The only one who can change your circumstances is YOU. Weigh what you long for against what is preventing you from having it. Once you have identified how you want to live and once you have figured out what distracts you from having that life, then it will be well worth doing whatever it takes. The power to change your own world lies within you.

Change is never easy. It requires you to confront your expectation, step out of your comfort zone, and take risks. You will probably make a few poor choices along the way. You might even fail a few times. When you do, you may view failure as "proof" that you are not good enough or smart enough to succeed, so you should just give up. Let that sink in for a minute. If we are ever to succeed at anything, we must first try.

As you begin to think about your life and changes you want or need to make, there are two points I would like you to consider:

1. Reframe the word "failure" as an opportunity to learn from your failure and mistakes. Every time you fail to achieve a goal, make a choice to learn and grow from it.

2. Failure stops us *only* if we let it stop us. It is important to pick yourself up and begin again every time you stumble.

Almost every successful person has experienced failure and doubt at some point, but they were not stopped by it. Many well-known celebrities turned failure into great successes:

- Michael Jordan was kicked off his high school basketball team because his coach didn't think his skills were good enough to play.
- Warren Buffet was rejected from attending Harvard University because his grades weren't good enough.
- Richard Branson was a high school dropout and was told he was likely to fail if he went to college.
- Martha Stewart greatly expanded her business empire after going to prison for 5 years.
- Oprah Winfrey was born into poverty to a teenage single mother and overcame numerous other challenges before becoming a beloved TV host and multibillionaire.

Those people that I mentioned are all famous household names. These others may not have the same immediate name recognition, but never the less, they built massive companies despite all odds:

- Kevin Plank, CEO of Under Armor, was almost broke when he began selling his signature athletic clothing.
- Barbara Corcoran, Real Estate Guru and Shark Tank celebrity, turned $1,000 into a billion dollar business.

* Andrew Carnegie spent the majority of his youth performing manual labor at a cotton mill. He built an empire in the railroad industry.

They all turned their failures or perceived failures into remarkable success stories that have inspired countless other people to follow their dreams. They each had a vision. They each set goals and had a plan. They intentionally lived a life they once could only dream of.

You will never know if you can have the life you dream of unless you try.

You can design your own life too if you face your fears and commit to doing what it takes to have what you say you want. If you want to accomplish anything worth having, you must start by taking action, even if they are baby steps. That will give you the drive and confidence you need to keep going. You will begin to see results and start gaining momentum.

When you take control of your life, you will start living life on your own terms and in your own unique style. You will experience a radical shift in mindset and momentum that will get you closer to living that life you once thought impossible. The more you live with intention, the easier it will be to embrace the one and only life you will ever have and live it to the fullest every day.

Lifestyle design allows you to create and design a life you were meant to live. The choices you make today will impact your tomorrows. The possibilities are endless. What are you waiting for?

If you really want a better life, why not start today? You can do it! Try it! You will discover a whole new confident, powerful, and unstoppable you.

In an effort to help you move forward so you can begin having the higher quality life you want, here are 10 steps you can take right now. As you begin to practice these steps, you will start to experience a greater sense of peace, confidence, well-being, and happiness. Once you realize that you can create anything you want for your life, you will become unstoppable.

10 Steps to Begin Living a Life You Love

1. **Try something new each day.** In Luann Cahn's Book, *I Dare Me*, she dared herself to try something new each day for an entire year. Having the courage to do this changed her thinking and her life.

2. **Learn something new.** Challenge your thinking. Change your world. Take a course, attend a seminar, and invest in your own personal growth and development.

3. **Surround yourself with people who are learning, growing, and challenging themselves to new heights.** Expand beyond what you ever thought possible. Grow in areas you want to know more about.

4. **Travel.** Take a trip to somewhere you've never been. Be inspired by discovering something new, immersing yourself in a whole new world.

5. **Lighten up!** Stop demanding perfection of yourself and others. Embrace imperfection. Take imperfect actions. You don't have to know all of the answers.

6. **Forgive yourself and others.** Stop letting what happened in the past hold you back. Put your

past in the past. Set yourself free from long-held upsets and resentments. You can't change the past, but you can change your future.

7. **Trust yourself.** Take risks. Learn from your mistakes. Embrace new opportunities that you would have previously stayed away from. Trust yourself to try some new skinny branches.

8. **Seek advice and opinions from other people who will only tell you the truth.** Learn from the experiences and wisdom of others. Get a mentor or trusted advisor who will provide new insights.

9. **Give back.** The more you give, the more you receive. Do something each day that will encourage, inspire or empower others to be their best self is your gift that will keep on giving.

10. **Live in the moment.** Each moment is an opportunity to create experiences and memories that will last your lifetime and beyond. Today will never come again.

THE SECOND ACT

Setting Your Stage

CHAPTER FOUR

Finding Your "Why"

"How finding your 'why' will help you find your way"

—JOHN MAXWELL

If someone were to ask, could you clearly articulate what touches you so deeply that it can actually move you to tears?

John Maxwell refers to this as "The why that makes you cry." In his book, *The Power of Significance*, he asserts that once you fully understand the reason you are here on this earth, your life will have meaning, hope, and significance. "Your why is what steers your ship even in life's roughest waters and it helps you stay in the game even when you are tempted to quit." When you intentionally live your purpose on purpose each day, that is a life well lived, a life of significance.

His process for discovering your why, your life purpose, consists of three questions well worth your time, effort, and contemplation.

- What do you cry about?
- What do you sing about?
- What do you dream about?

WHAT DO YOU CRY ABOUT?

Recently, I woke up from a deep sleep, sobbing uncontrollably. I had been dreaming about a homeless woman I befriended in Philadelphia last winter. I met her at a stoplight when she approached my car in her wheelchair requesting food, clothing, or money. Having lived in the city for a while, I was used to being approached by the homeless, so I keep small gift bags of food, gloves, socks and scarves in my car. I handed her the pretty bag with a few things in it. She clutched it to her heart and thanked me for the Christmas present and wished me a merry Christmas. Since that time, even in the short time it takes for a red light to turn green, I have come to know more about Hannah. I actually look forward to getting a red light so I have an opportunity to talk to her.

In July, I realized I hadn't seen her in several weeks and became concerned, but I also had no way of contacting her or anyone else who might know of her whereabouts. So each time I came to that stoplight, I said a prayer for her. Then, a few weeks ago, I was excited to see her back on her corner. She waved and smiled brightly as she rolled her wheelchair towards my car window. She quickly explained that she had passed out during one of the hot summer days and fell out of her wheelchair onto the road. Rushed to the emergency room, she was admitted for several days, then released back to her "home" on the streets. When I told her I was concerned that I hadn't seen her, she thanked me, saying, "No one is ever concerned about me." That statement broke my heart.

Hannah's story is what made me cry. I couldn't stop thinking about it. It moved me so deeply that my homeless, disabled friend who lives on the street corner, who begs for life's most basic needs, endured that frightening moment alone. As I sat up in bed thinking about it, I realized it was my why that had me cry. For years, I have known that my passion and purpose is to help women who are hurting and afraid. Why? Because several times in my life I was that woman who was alone, hurting and afraid. Those experiences formed my commitment to helping women empower themselves to have a fresh start. While my friend, Hannah, resisted my offer to help her find an apartment, I vowed to continue the conversation. As a result of those tears about Hannah's plight, I was inspired to commit a percentage of my book proceeds to go towards women like Hannah who need a hand-up, a place to live, and a friend so they never feel alone again.

In other words, what touches you so deeply that it moves you to tears? It could be something that breaks your heart and maybe even causes you to feel a deep pain inside. It also motivates you to take action to bring healing, change and to make a difference.

What Do You Cry About?

* Recall moments in your life that you were so deeply touched that you were compelled to take action.

* Reconnect with where you were, time of day, who you were with, and what happened.

* Relive the experience. The sites, the sounds, the smells.

* Describe in detail what it was that moved you so deeply.

WHAT DO YOU SING ABOUT?

♦ Has there been a time in your life where you jumped out of bed so excited to take on your day?

♦ What is it that makes you so happy that you could literally jump for joy?

♦ Think of the last time you were in your "zone."
  ♦ Time stopped.
  ♦ Nothing else mattered.
  ♦ You were hyper focused, motivated, and intentional.
  ♦ There was nothing on earth you would have rather been doing.

If you are asking yourself these types of questions, you are already on the path to discovering what you sing about, what your passions are. Asking yourself questions like these will help you discern what inspires you. Create a journal where you can keep a record of your journey and begin to see red threads that connect the dots to what lights you up.

The process takes time. It is a journey. It will evolve and unfold over time. You are a work in progress.

When your innate talents and strengths intersect with your passion, you are more productive, you find value, meaning and fulfillment. It is the moment your life and work align with who you are and what you care about most. It is when you do your best work.

Knowing what makes you sing is integral to living a life you love. It will make you rethink everything you do by helping you focus more of your time, energy, and attention to those things that light you up like nothing else can. It will drive you to take risks, think out of the box, and try things that are difficult, even seemingly impossible to accomplish. Knowing what makes you sing will inspire you to believe in yourself, own your power and voice, and stimulate you to take action so that you can have more of what you really want in life.

Discovering that sweet spot, when you are in your zone, when you feel more alive, more productive is when you're using your God-given talents each day to contribute not just to your own life but also to others. It is living in alignment with what matters most to you and what you are committed to in your life.

The moment I stood on the TEDx stage to deliver the talk of my life, "Downsize your life, why less is more," I realized I was doing what made me sing… what gave me life and renewed my energy. It was when I knew I could make a difference on a much larger scale to empower others to discover the life they love by living with less.

Take time to discern what it is that makes you come alive, what feeds your soul and lights you up.

- What are your innate strengths?
- Where can you add the greatest value?
- What are you most committed to in your life?

How would you answer this statement? Nothing makes me happier than when I am (you fill in the blank). For me, nothing makes me happier than when I am helping people discover how they can live the life they love.

What Do You Sing About?

Notice:
- Small things that light you up.
- Conversations or experiences that excite you.
- Events or opportunities that you look forward to.

Listen:
- To what you are drawn to.
- To what you love doing and who you love being with.
- To what feeds your soul and provides deep satisfaction and meaning.

Be open to:
- Discovering what makes you sing in each area of your life, including work, relationships, family, finances, spiritual, personal and professional development and fun.

WHAT DO YOU DREAM ABOUT?

As an interior designer, I encourage my clients to allow themselves to dream, to expand their thinking way beyond what they ever thought possible within their budget. Our "Signature Magic of Three Design Process" offers 3 uniquely different design concepts. It helps our clients step out of their comfort zone and embrace thinking out of their own box. During this creative process, we ask that for the moment they remove all constraints of money, time, resources, etc. This opens them up to possibilities they might never have considered before. We help them dream and visualize what is possible.

For me, this is one of the most exciting parts of the design process because they are not constrained by thinking about what holds them back. It allows us to help them "see through walls" and beyond what they could see before.

As a lifestyle designer and lifestyle coach, I help people "see through walls", overcome barriers and obstacles that prevent them from dreaming and believing they can actually design a life they want, desire, and deserve.

"BEST CHRISTMAS EVER"

Several years ago, I met with a new client who shared with me that they had succeeded in getting their three children through college and it was now time to have the kitchen they had dreamed about for many years. They had put their dream kitchen on hold until they no longer had college expenses.

When I asked them to tell me about their dream kitchen, they proceeded to describe a new look, new appliances, and new lighting within their existing space. When I started to ask questions about how often they used their adjoining dining room, they responded, "three times per year." I then asked them if they would consider bumping through that wall to double the size of their existing kitchen. They were excited about that possibility.

Then pushing even more boundaries, I asked them what they thought of partially opening another wall into their family/ TV room.

I will never forget their response, "You mean so that we can all be together?"

When I said that was definitely possible, I could see the excitement on their faces… their big dreams just got bigger! And it was possible within the budget they allotted.

Their kitchen renovation was completed a week before Christmas. Several weeks after the holiday season, I stopped by to drop off a small gift. I was greeted with huge hugs and both of them saying, "This was the best Christmas ever." When I asked them why, they said, "We were all finally able to be together. No longer separated by walls."

What mattered most to them, their big dream, was to have their family be together.

Part of our interior design process is to help our clients "see through walls" to help them see what is possible without being constrained by past-based thinking. We help them to see beyond what they think is possible and then make it happen.

As a lifestyle designer, I also help people "see through walls," barriers, and obstacles that prevent them from dreaming about what they want most in life.

- For many people, the number one challenge is that they simply do not know what they want.
- Others choose to just let life happen.
- Still, others have either given up on their dreams or believe it's not possible to have a life they really want.

According to a survey by Forbes, when asked what they want "more of" in life, people responded in this order:

1. Happiness
2. Money
3. Freedom
4. Joy
5. Balance
6. Fulfillment
7. Confidence
8. Stability
9. Passion
10. Purpose

Putting any of these on hold or thinking they are not possible is simply not true. If we truly want something in our life, it is possible and it all begins with a dream. True, dreaming might scare you and it can definitely push you out of your comfort zone, but if it is a wish or a dream, it is deep within your heart. It all begins with a dream and a vision for what you want most, what you are yearning for, believing that you can have it.

Life is a choice.

Either accept the status quo or go after what you really want, what you dream of. Don't be afraid to say it out loud, write it down, make a plan, and implement it over time. Even baby steps count.

Allow yourself to dream, to choose the way your life goes.

A question we all got asked when we were children: "What do you want to be when you grow up?" You might have responded: astronaut, scientist, doctor, teacher...

What happened to our ability to dream big dreams like we did when we were children?

What stops us? I encourage you to be curious, wonder, dream about, and visualize the life you most want, starting right now.

DESIRED OUTCOMES

Use the following exercise to explore these desired outcomes:

- Clarity about what matters most to you, what fuels your passion and desires.
- Believe that you can choose to live your life of purpose on purpose, a life filled with meaning.
- Believe you can live the life you love, one of significance and great impact.

- Commit to specific goals, plan, and actions that you can take to have and live the life you love. Practice seeing your life through the new lens of what you cry about, what you sing about and what you dream about.

Perhaps, your dream involves significant changes:

- Quitting a dead-end job
- Terminating toxic relationships
- Moving closer to your children and grandchildren
- Downsizing to a smaller home
- Travel to bucket-list places

What Do You Dream About?

- Make a list of what you dream about and wish you had in all areas of your life. Recall dreams you may have forgotten and those you may have completely given up on.

    - Relationships
    - Family
    - Career/ Business
    - Finances
    - Personal and Professional Development
    - Spirituality
    - Health

- For the moment remove all constraints, barriers, obstacles and negative thinking that prevents you from attaining your dreams and the life you really want. This list should include constraints like time, money, resources, energy, opportunity, and experiences.

- Dream. Dream bigger. If you could do, be, or realize your dreams, how would your life change?

START WITH "WHY"

Simon Sinek's TED Talk, "Start with Why" is ranked among the top 3 greatest TED talks of all time. In his talk, he said, "If you know your why, you will figure out how."

Our life has meaning, fulfillment, and purpose when our decisions, goals, and actions are inspired by and aligned with our values, passions, and God-given talents.

Knowing our why, our life purpose, is like a GPS that allows us to focus and direct our actions toward what matters most to us in our lives. Life is easier and much more fun when we are clear and confident about who we are and what we can uniquely contribute to the world. We believe we can make a difference and we know that what we do matters.

When we live with purpose each day...

+ We are more engaged and connected.
+ We have more energy and look forward to doing more and being more.
+ We are more fulfilled, rewarded, and satisfied.
+ We have more opportunities available.
+ We become unstoppable.

Once you discover and can clearly articulate your life purpose, you are empowered and in control of your own life. You choose how and where your life will go. You get to design and live the life you love, which connects to you, the authentic you. It is an opportunity to find happiness, beauty, meaning and fulfillment each day. You are lit up, inspired, and motivated to live life to the fullest and make a difference. You have given yourself permission to dream, explore, create, and thrive.

You will forget when you are not connected to your why, when life was hard, when you allowed life to just happen to you, when you were not in control of your own destiny. There was no GPS. You were floundering and you were lost.

If you are still not sure what your life purpose is, I encourage you to not settle for a mediocre status quo kind of life that has no compass that leads to your North Star. Start where you are. Take baby steps. Today.

- Listen to what you cry about, sing about, and dream about.
- Give yourself permission to listen deeply to your feelings, to connect with who you are now and who you want to be in the future.
- If you don't know or are having difficulty figuring out your why or your life purpose, you are not alone. It takes time; just keep listening to what you yearn for.

You too can live a life of purpose on purpose. It's not just for a chosen few. When you discover what matters most to you, what you value and don't, you too will find your why that makes you cry.

You Are Ready Now
Whether You Know It Or Not

• Even if you can't clearly articulate your why yet, take small steps by living each day in alignment with what you care most about.

• Start by doing more of what you love and less of what you don't.

• It takes time to discern and discover your purpose. Be patient.

You Are Evolving, So is Your Life Purpose

• As our lives change, and as we transition into a new phase of our lives, what we cry about, sing about and dream about also changes. (i.e. empty nest, retirement, divorced, widowed)

• New possibilities emerge, allowing our life purpose to evolve and expand to take on new meaning that is satisfying and fulfilling.

Our purpose reveals itself when we stop being afraid and when we start being our authentic selves. Unlocking our purpose is wisdom and insight that is created by life experiences over periods of time.

Don't wait to design and live the life you love. Live your purpose on purpose. Right now. It's never too late.

CHAPTER FIVE

Downsizing from the Inside Out

"Our unopened boxes are our brain's version of our to-do list."
—STEPHEN COVEY

- Do you still have unopened boxes from your last move? Boxes that are still sitting unopened in your basement, garage, attic or storage unit?
- Do you have any idea what's inside of them?
- Have you ever asked yourself why you brought so many more things from your previous home than what you actually needed?

The reality is that many of us probably do have unopened boxes and we have also probably forgotten what is inside. And likely, we wonder why we even brought them in the first place. Even though I radically downsized myself two years ago, I am guilty of still having numerous unopened boxes in my storage unit. Yes, a storage unit that I pay for each month to store my excess stuff that I either couldn't part with or that didn't fit in my tiny apartment.

A few months ago, I was preparing a speech for an audience of baby boomers interested in downsizing and decluttering. Just for fun, I challenged myself to go to my storage unit and open one of those mysterious boxes because that's what I was going to challenge my audience to do.

Here is what I found in that unopened box:

- Twelve unopened VHS tapes and cassettes on motivational speaking.
- Report cards from my sons' elementary school when teachers actually wrote grades and comments by hand.
- My son's high school soccer shorts that still smelled!
- A macaroni picture frame that one of my sons made in preschool.
- The set of car keys I had been looking for and that I thought were lost.

Here's what I discovered about myself:

- The VHS tapes and cassettes were visual reminders that I aspired to become a national speaker *someday*. They were still wrapped in cellophane, unopened. I wasn't ready to become a speaker at that time of my life, but I aspired to it. Today, I speak to audiences all over the country on the impact of downsizing and living with less.
- The report cards, soccer shorts, and macaroni picture frame were visual reminders of special times in my life that I was afraid of losing. I thought that if I got rid of

those "precious" items, I would also lose those priceless memories.

+ I took pictures of each of them, put them in a Shutterfly album as fun and funny reminders of those special years of raising my sons. When I called my son to let him know that I had found his prized soccer shorts, he laughed out loud and gave me "permission" to let them go! The macaroni picture frame and report cards were sweet memories, but no longer needed as reminders of that special time in my life.

+ I threw them away without tears or regret. I was ready to let go.

+ As for the extra set of car keys... well, that was just good luck that I finally found them! I kept them because I needed them!

After opening the box and dealing with each item in it, I was not only able to let go of the physical item itself but also the emotional attachment I had been holding on to.

Have you ever wondered why you brought so much more than was needed from your last home? If you are considering downsizing, are you beginning to rethink how much you will actually want and need?

This might sound a little radical, and even harsh, especially to those of you who are experiencing not only the physical drain of downsizing but also the emotional aspect... the stress and overwhelm.

Downsizing your physical space might actually be the easiest part of your entire downsizing journey.

We have busy and cluttered lives:

- Too many commitments, too much stuff.
- Too many "should's" and "have-to's."
- Too few boundaries.
- Not enough time or energy for things that matter most to us.

But it is not just the physical clutter that devours our time and pervades our homes and work places. It is also the mental and emotional clutter that fills our minds, causing stress, an overwhelming feeling, and anxiety, which diminishes and detracts from the quality of our lives each day.

It is the inside clutter, the emotional clutter, that causes the much bigger downsizing and decluttering challenge. This is what prevents us from making room for the life we most want... the life we can actually have if we take the time to deal with the inside emotional clutter that prevents us from having the life we want and deserve!

OUR UNOPENED BOXES

Think back to the unopened boxes in your basement and garage:

- Why did you take too much stuff with you in the first place?
- Why was it so difficult to let go of certain items?
- Why have they remained unopened?

Perhaps, it was *guilt* that you inherited a family heirloom that meant so much to a lost loved one. Perhaps, you felt you would disrespect your grandmother if you gave away her favorite lounge chair or china cabinet.

OR

Perhaps, it was *fear* of letting go of something you worked long and hard for... that college diploma or marathon medal.

OR

Perhaps, it was *sentimental* and reminded you of a special time in your life... the well-worn teddy bear or child's blanket.

According to Steven Covey, all of the unopened boxes are a metaphor for what we still need to acknowledge and deal with in our lives, the still unfinished business.

- ♦ They are visual reminders of what is left undone in our lives.
- ♦ They are reminders of decisions we either chose to not make or failed to make before we moved.
- ♦ They are unopened, hidden from our sight so they don't need to be dealt with. Out of sight, out of mind.
- ♦ They remain unopened, concerned that we might need it *someday*.
- ♦ They were not a priority, so they were left to be dealt with at a later time.

IS IT TIME TO OPEN THE BOXES AND MAKE ROOM FOR THE LIFE YOU WANT?

If you are not living the life you want right now, what *unopened boxes* do you need to deal with to free yourself up to live more fully?

As you begin your downsizing journey, downsizing the mental and emotional clutter is equally important to downsizing and decluttering your physical possessions and space. Look at what is preventing you from having the life you dream about—the one you say you are committed to having. Perhaps, it is time to develop an awareness of your unconscious beliefs, your old patterns of thinking and destructive self-sabotaging habits that influence our behavior, actions, and overall quality of life.

So is it time to open those boxes that have been hidden from your view so that you can better understand how to let go, move forward, and live the life you are meant to live?

Make it a priority to deal with your unfinished business so you will have space for an amazing life.

Downsizing from the inside out
SELF–ASSESSMENT

1. How are these emotions holding you back from having the life you really want?

   ◆ Guilt
   ◆ Resentment
   ◆ Lack of forgiveness
   ◆ Shame
   ◆ Anger
   ◆ Other

2. How does fear get in your way?

   ◆ Fear of failure
   ◆ Fear of rejection
   ◆ Fear of success
   ◆ Fear of not doing it right

3. What do you consistently put off until tomorrow? (Procrastinate)

4. When you are "stuck," what small steps can you take to get unstuck so you can move forward?

CHAPTER SIX

Making Room for the Life You Really Want

"Life has no limitations except the ones you make."

–LES BROWN

Marcie was running late for an important business meeting, but she almost didn't care. She was stuck in a job she hated, one that sucked energy from every cell in her body. She had worked at the same accounting firm for twenty two years, was a well-respected partner, and one of the top performers in her company.

But none of that mattered to her anymore. She was simply putting in time to collect a paycheck so that she could retire comfortably, travel, and live the life she dreamed of having… *someday*. No one knew what she dreamed of. Why would she share her innermost desires with anyone? They wouldn't understand and they would certainly not care. All that mattered to them was that she performed well in her job, made money for her company, and that she received a nice paycheck at the end of every week.

Marcie was resigned to believing her life would always be that way. She had no expectations that she could actually change her circumstances and alter the direction of her life to have what she really wanted AND a good job that would be fulfilling and financially rewarding. She limited her own happiness and personal satisfaction by choosing a status quo existence. She had convinced herself that she was stuck in a job she detested until one day she would retire and be magically in love with life.

She also never questioned if that was all there was and if it had to be that way. She was stuck, but not so much in the job, as in her own thinking that prevented her from having what she dreamed of every day.

If you are not living the life you really want right now, if you are not getting the joy, happiness and satisfaction you want in any area of your life (career, finances, relationship, personal growth), then begin to ask yourself these three important life-changing questions:

+ What kind of life do you dream of and long for?
+ What is preventing you from living that life right now?
+ How can you change your current thinking, beliefs, behaviors, and habits to make room for the life you really want?

As discussed in previous chapters, lifestyle design is living intentionally in all areas of your life, living in alignment with what matters most to you so you can live a life you love every day, *starting now*. Lifestyle design involves choices. How you choose to spend your precious time, resources, energy, and God-given talents matters.

Perhaps Marcie didn't believe she had a choice to stop working in a job she despised, one that influenced her overall wellbeing and happiness. Perhaps she wasn't even aware that her thinking and mindset were holding her back. Awareness is key to understanding what prevents and stops us. But then after that, it is up to us to choose and pursue a life we really want.

5 THINGS THAT PREVENT YOU FROM HAVING THE LIFE YOU REALLY WANT

1. Self-limiting beliefs
2. Scarcity mindset vs. abundant mindset
3. Fixed mindset vs growth mindset
4. Destructive, self-sabotaging habits
5. "Should's" and "Have-to's"

1. SELF-LIMITING BELIEFS

When it comes to designing an incredible life, there are no limits to what you can do or what you can have. The only thing keeping you from having the life you *really* want is you and not believing you can have it. These self-limiting beliefs appear in many ways.

Can you relate to any of the following statements?

- I'm afraid to pursue my dreams because I might fail again.
- I will never have the relationships that I want because I'm afraid to get hurt again.
- I'm afraid of being rejected, so I don't ask for what I want.
- I'm afraid people will judge me, so I don't speak up and use my voice.

- It's too late; I'm too old to pursue my dreams.
- I can't possibly do that... I'm not smart enough.
- I will never have what I really want because I don't deserve that.

The sad thing is, when you start to look closely at these self-limiting beliefs, none of them are actually true. They are simply something we have told ourselves over and over again until we believe they are true. When we accept these as part of our daily internal dialogue, then those beliefs become part of us, our own personal truth. They become part of what we believe about ourselves and that is what stops us from pursuing our dreams and being all that we can be.

The other sad thing is that much of what we tell ourselves stemmed from something that happened in our past. Whatever happened in that moment, we made a decision about ourselves that limits us to this day.

In seventh grade, my older brother, Ed, was asked to give a report in front of the class. In giving his report, he was nervous and made a mistake. His class laughed at him, and as he tells it, he made a decision in that moment that he would never speak in public again. Fortunately, years later, he decided to overcome his fear of public speaking and started a business helping others push through their own self-limiting beliefs that they are not smart enough to speak in public. He now impacts people all over the country who use their voices to make a difference in the world.

Think about it. At this stage of our lives, who hasn't experienced being laughed at, or being judged? Who hasn't experienced heartbreak or failure? Of course, these negative experiences had an impact on us, but why do we continue to let them hold us back?

It is important to consistently challenge our self-limiting beliefs and ways of thinking that hold us back. What you believe about yourself, your abilities, and what you are capable of achieving can actually be a predictor of how successful you will live your life.

- If you believe you can accomplish great things, you will.
- If you believe you can have a great life, you are probably right.

Conversely, if you don't believe you can accomplish great things or have a great life, you are probably right.

While there are certainly things in life you cannot change (like your past experiences), what you can control are your beliefs about who you are and who you are capable of becoming. It makes sense then that since your self-beliefs are that powerful and influential, you might consider doing everything you can to counteract limiting beliefs. Instead, empower yourself to believe you can be all you want to be and so much more.

This is not to say that those same self-limiting beliefs and fears will not continue to resurface. The power and the magic is to become aware of them so that when they do appear you can choose to respond differently and more powerfully than you have in the past. By becoming aware of what triggers you, you can alter your behavior. The choice becomes yours to make.

It is difficult to believe that someone who is as admired as Oprah has had to deal with her own self-limiting beliefs about her being big, beautiful and successful. In an effort to understand her own limiting belief system, she remembered a time when she was on the scale weighing herself. Her father walked by and said that there was no need for her to weigh herself because she would always be big like her mother. Oprah came to believe that she couldn't be beautiful, big, and successful. The rest is history.

HOW TO OVERCOME YOUR
SELF-LIMITING BELIEFS

* **Know that you have them.**
  Write the beliefs that are holding you back down. (E.g., I'm not smart enough to speak in front of a large audience.)

* **Discern the reasons why you believe what you do.**
  What experiences did you have in the past that has you believe that about yourself? (E.g., I don't deserve the raise that I really want and need.)

* **Recognize that these beliefs are just a story you told yourself.**
  Our brain protects us from experiencing pain or embarrassment, so it tells us not to do it. (E.g., I will be laughed at or judged by an audience if I speak.)

* **Choose new and empowering beliefs about yourself.**
  Reprogram your thinking by creating new positive, empowering beliefs about yourself (E.g., I am an inspiring, confident, public speaker. My audience cares about what I have to say.)

2. SCARCITY MINDSET VS. ABUNDANT MINDSET

If only...

* You had more money, a bigger house or a better job.
* You lost 30 pounds, were trim and fit and healthier.
* You had more time, more experience, an advanced degree.

Then...

* Your life would be easier and better.
* You would be more attractive to the man of your dreams.
* You would have less stress and be happier.

Do you have similar thoughts? Are you often focused on what you don't' have? This scarcity mindset keeps us feeling stuck, preventing us from having a life we really want. It limits possibility while abundant thinking focuses on what we do have, allowing us to be grateful and see possibility and opportunity in our lives.

Notice how each of these mindsets might show up in your life:

Scarcity Mindset:

* Your glass is always half empty.
* You never seem to have enough time, money or opportunity.
* You focus on your limitations.
* You think and dream small.
* You avoid risks at all costs.
* You experience fear, anger, frustration, resentment and anxiety.
* You compete to stay on top.
* You are insecure when others succeed.
* You see yourself as not good enough, smart enough, deserving enough.

Abundant Mindset:

- Your glass is always at least half full.
- You have enough time, money, and opportunity.
- You focus on creating new opportunities.
- You think and dream big.
- You embrace risk.
- You are courageous, curious, calm, happy and content.
- You are grateful and generous with your time, money and talent.
- You are inspired by the success of others.
- You embrace failure as part of learning, growing and changing.

A *scarcity* mindset imprisons you and prevents you from living life fully.

An *abundant* mindset liberates you and provides an opportunity to live a happier, more fulfilling life, where you believe the rest of your life can be the best of your life.

Shifting from a scarcity mindset to one of abundance is a choice. Surround yourself with people who think and live abundantly and model their mindset and behavior.

Health and Wellness. If you want to lose weight, find someone you admire who has lost weight and successfully kept it off. Or if you want to be trim and fit, seek out friends who have a fitness regime that fits the healthy lifestyle you aspire to.

Relationships. If you want a loving partner and relationship, listen and learn from couples who have a long happy marriage or committed partnership. Observe and emulate ways they communicate and collaborate with each other.

Career. If you want to become a great motivational speaker, seek training and coaching from those who have successful speaking businesses and careers. Create opportunities to speak and practice.

How to Have an Abundant and Empowering Mindset in Every Area of Your Life

Choose gratitude and enough.
- Remind yourself of all you do have and be thankful for it.
- Focus on having enough and being enough.
- Focus on what you have already accomplished.

Celebrate the success of others.
- Know that there is plenty to go around.
- Be inspired by them, be happy for them.
- In turn, your success will inspire others.

Create opportunities to grow, learn and change.
- Practice dreaming bigger, thinking bigger.
- Take risks.
- Embrace your failures, setbacks, and disappointments. Consider them as opportunities to grow and learn.

If you are committed to making the room for the life you really want, downsize your scarcity mindset and upgrade to your new abundant mindset and lifestyle.

3. FIXED MINDSET VS. GROWTH MINDSET

The following statements represent two completely different views of life and how people see and operate in the world.

Fixed Mindset

- I'm fine with the way things are. I don't need or want to change.
- I'm doing the best I can.
- It's just the way I am.
- It's just the way life is.
- There is nothing I can do that will change anything.

Growth Mindset

- That's the way my life is right now but I want to improve it so I can have the life I really want.
- I'm willing to do what it takes to have the life I want.
- I realize that change does not happen overnight, so I am willing to do the hard work.
- Over time, I will have the life I really want.
- I have a choice. I am choosing to invest my time, money and effort to have a life I love.

If you see life through the lens of a *fixed mindset*, you are born with basic, innate qualities like intelligence and talent. You believe these are fixed traits.

If you see life through the lens of a *growth mindset*, you believe your most basic abilities can be developed, improved and expanded upon, which creates a love of learning, new experiences, and persistence. The benefit of a growth mindset seems obvious, but most of us have a fixed mindset in certain situations.

Perhaps, you can identify with some of these *fixed mindset* statements:

- I'm not good at... (math, technology)
- I can't... (change a tire, draw)

- I'm bad at… (singing, dancing)
- I don't want to learn … (a new language, how to change the oil in my car)

The fixed mindset can prevent us from developing skills that could sabotage personal and professional growth. For example, if you say, "I'm not good at managing money or making money," then that belief acts as an easy excuse to avoid becoming adept at earning, saving, and investing. The fixed mindset prevents you from failing in the short term, but in the long term, it hinders your ability to learn, grow, and develop valuable life skills.

Conversely, if you say, "This is something I'm not currently good at, but I realize how important it is for me to learn and develop expertise in the area of my finances." People with the growth mindset learn how to overcome challenges rather than avoid them. They are inspired by opportunity to grow and learn.

EXAMPLES OF A FIXED MINDSET AND A GROWTH MINDSET

WORK

Fixed: You hate your job, but you have to work to earn money. You are miserable, frustrated, and angry, yet you do nothing about it but complain.

Growth: Because I need a secure, well-paying job right now to pay college bills, I am trying to find ways to make my current job more interesting, challenging and fun until I ultimately find the job I love and plenty of income.

HOME

Fixed: I really want to move to a smaller home now that my kids are grown, but I'm overwhelmed at the thought of downsizing and have no idea where to start.

Growth: If I really want to move to a smaller, more manageable and affordable home that provides the new and exciting lifestyle that I want, I will create a plan and form a team so I can make my downsizing a reality.

RELATIONSHIP

Fixed: We've been married for so long and even though there's no excitement and spark anymore, at least I know I won't grow old alone. I don't know how to reignite our relationship, so I'm just going to stick it out.

Growth: I'm so grateful to be married to a man I still love after forty years. He is still the love of my life and I am going to remind him of that every day. I can hardly wait to see what happens.

FINANCES

Fixed: You are in debt. You have no savings. You are concerned about your future. You are anxious, overwhelmed, yet you continue to spend.

Growth: Even though I may not have saved enough for retirement, I will create a lucrative part-time business that I love. It will supplement my savings and income so that I can have a financially secure retirement.

TIME

Fixed: You never seem to have enough time for family, friends or yourself. You are just too busy, you are overwhelmed, stressed and miserable.

Growth: I value and respect myself, so I choose to create time not just for my family and friends but also for myself. I powerfully say no and create boundaries that respect my own wants, needs, and wish list.

POSSESSIONS

Fixed: I know I have too much stuff and yet I keep buying more because it makes me happy for at least a little while.

Growth: I take responsibility for buying and owning too much stuff. I am taking actions to curb my spending and discern why I bought so much in the first place.

PHYSICAL CLUTTER

Fixed: I can't find anything. I'm overwhelmed and have no idea how to organize and get rid of my stuff.

Growth: Enough! Today, I am going to begin the process of decluttering my home and office. I know it will take time and likely be emotional to let go of things that have meaning, but it will be worth having a clutter-free environment and peace of mind.

EMOTIONAL CLUTTER

Fixed: I carry so much anger, resentment, guilt, and shame around with me each day. I know it's preventing me from moving on with my life but I am not willing to change my thinking.

Growth: It's time for me to let go of past hurts, abuse, disappointment and failures. I struggle with this and don't know how to let go, so I will be reaching out for some professional assistance. It matters to me so I can move on with my life.

TECHNOLOGY/ SOCIAL MEDIA

Fixed: I think I'm addicted to my devices. They take valuable time away from my family, but my family is addicted too. We do not spend quality time together.

Growth: Today, I am taking control of the amount of time I spend on the internet and social media. Nothing means more to me than my family. It is up to me to prioritize quality time with them and be a good role model.

SELF-LIMITING BELIEFS

Fixed: I'm not smart enough to create my own company that would provide the kind of lifestyle I want. Other people make it seem so easy. I won't event try because I know I will fail.

Growth: Every time I hear that little voice in my head that say, "I'm not smart enough," I'm going to use a whack-a-mole tool that I learned to smack it back down. I'm smart enough to have anything that I want and I'm willing to work hard to get it.

HOW TO DEVELOP A GROWTH MINDSET

- Replace the word failing with the word learning. When you make a mistake or fall short of a goal, you haven't failed but you have learned.

- Enjoy the process over the end results. Value the process and opportunity to learn; it is a journey.

- Keep the big picture in mind. Emphasize growth over speed.

- Stop comparing yourself to others. Learn to seek approval from yourself rather than others.

- Learn to take risks regularly. Accept that you will fail sometimes.

When you downsize your fixed mindset and upgrade to a growth mindset, your world view changes to provide a higher quality of life, one that is more meaningful and fulfilling.

4. DESTRUCTIVE AND SELF-SABOTAGING HABITS

Habits are unconscious behaviors that we do without even being aware of them. They are the foundation of our everyday lives. Our daily practices, habits, and routines shape us. Our good habits support us and help us accomplish our goals. Our bad habits are destructive and undermine our capacity and potential to execute and obtain our desired results. As the saying goes, "bad habits die hard." But if you want to make room for the life you love, it's important to look at habits through a new lens of how they might be holding you back.

How might your self-sabotaging habits be impacting your life and preventing you from a having a life you really want?

Distinguish what you might want and need to D clutter and or downsize on the inside to help you improve the quality of your life on the outside.

The need to always be perfect:

Accept that we are good at some things and not as good at others. When expectations are too high, we are afraid to make mistakes and therefore might not take the chance to even try.

Waiting for the perfect time to start:

Fear of moving forward means you may never start. There is no perfect time. If you never start, you will never succeed.

Not letting go:

It's difficult to walk away from something you have invested in emotionally and financially. Learning to let go will give you the freedom to move on and seek other opportunities.

Overspending or not having a budget:

Mindless and careless spending can seriously undermine chances for a secure future. There is also a great deal of anxiety associated with overspending and debt.

Staying in your comfort zone (not taking risks):

Risk can be scary. It can also be very exciting. It means the possibility of failure, but it also means the possibility of success.

Talking negatively about yourself and others:

Your inner critic invites negative thoughts about yourself and your abilities. Wounds that are inflicted upon others can bring irreparable harm.

Lack of focus:

Allowing distractions to pull you away from life goals inhibits growth.

Inaction:

Failure to move forward or fear of taking the next step prevents growth.

Self-doubt:

Self-doubt kills dreams. Fear of rejection, negative self-talk invites uncertainty and indecision. It is self-perpetuating.

Neglecting health:

Overeating, lack of exercise, and not getting enough sleep lead to exhaustion, negative impact on performance, emotional and physical issues and lack of productivity.

Lack of direction and undefined goals:

The need for a vision and clearly defined goals or a plan helps you to stay on course to accomplish these goals.

Need for approval:

Making what others think of you more important than what you think of you is debilitating.

Shifting the blame:

Making excuses, not accepting responsibility for things when they go wrong.

Busyness:

Has busyness become your mantra? Are you too busy *doing* that you don't make time to enjoy the experience of being in the present moment?

Multi-tasking:

Do you say yes to too many things in your life? Do you try to do it all even if you don't want to?

Naysayers:

Do you have people in your life who consistently say you can't so you can stop believing you can?

Other types of self-sabotaging and destructive habits:

* Always running late
* Clutter, physical and emotional
* Not listening

Some habits are debilitating and we might not even realize how much they are impacting us. Simply being aware of how they are influencing our lives can be a step in the right direction.

How to rewire your behavior to change bad habits:

+ Identify the habit (i.e. overeating)

+ Identify the reward you get from your habit (i.e. temporary relief from stress because it tastes good).

+ Imagine that you have the power to control and change and habit (i.e. when you are frustrated, stressed, angry or feeling underappreciated).

+ Develop an awareness of times that you revert back to the habit (i.e. overeating).

+ Understand why you revert back to the habit (i.e. feel powerless, upset, hurt, etc.).

+ Consciously choose one behavior at a time and substitute it with a positive behavior.

It takes approximately twenty one days to rewire your behavior pattern. It's well worth the effort to change. There is no magic bullet that will change these habitual behaviors overnight. But if you want to make a difference in the quality of your life, it's important to downsize bad habits and upgrade them to good habits that will enhance your new lifestyle.

5. The should's and have-tos:

"I'm not in this world to live up to your expectations and you're not in this world to live up to mine." Unknown

Many people feel pressured by the expectations of others and outside forces. This causes them to feel frustrated, miserable, and confused about what they want for themselves. Measuring yourself by others' expectations is a sure-fire way to diminish your own self-worth.

Do you find yourself spending far more time pleasing others, fulfilling their expectations of you (the way you *should* dress, the school you *should* attend, the profession you *should* go into)? When will you start taking control of your own life? Are there too many *"have-to's"* and not enough *"want-to's"* on your schedule? These are all within your control. You just need to boldly hold your ground, based on what matters and doesn't matter to you. Be committed to the following: no means no. Yes means yes. Your boundaries set expectations and limits for you and others. It's your life, not theirs.

MAKE ROOM FOR THE LIFE YOU REALLY WANT

Explore these five things that might be preventing you from having the life you most want:

- **Clarity** about what you most want and making it a priority.
- **Clarity** about what is preventing you from having that.
- **Choose** only what is in alignment with what matters most to you.
- **Reframe** your conversation to only those that empower you.
- **Set boundaries** and limits on anything that distracts you from having the life you want.

SELF-ASSESSMENT

Use this list to distinguish how these might be preventing you from having the life you really want, impacting the quality of your life.

1. **Self-limiting beliefs**

   How do your self-limiting beliefs prevent you from living fully?

2. **Scarcity mindset**

   How does not having enough or being enough stop you?

3. **Fixed mindset**

   Do you hear yourself saying, "I can't, I won't, I don't want to?" How does this prevent you from being open to new opportunity?

4. **Destructive Habits**

   What destructive habits prevent you from living your life more fully?

5. **Should's and Have-to's**

   How do you allow the expectations of others overshadow your own wants and needs?

THE THIRD ACT

Make the Rest of your Life
the Best of your Life

CHAPTER SEVEN

Waking Up

I was at a stoplight. The phone rang, I picked it up and heard my brother say, "Dad had a massive stroke but he is still alive." Time stopped. My rock, my dad, might die. I need to see him, to be with him. Now. But he was six hours away.

Car? Plane? Train was the best and safest option. I drove to the train station, making arrangements with my ex-husband to care for our young boys so I could get to Rhode Island and be with my dad and my siblings. I sat next to a window at the rear of the train, crying uncontrollably. A woman got on the train in Philadelphia and asked if she could sit next to me. Seeing that I was crying, she asked if she could help. I blurted out that my dad had just had a massive stroke and I was trying to get to Rhode Island to see him in time. She reached over, gently touched my arm and said, "You are lucky. He is still living." I was stunned by her words, "You are lucky." She continued, "Just a few months ago, my dad had a massive stroke and died instantly." She said I was lucky because it was still possible that I could see him. As harsh as it may have sounded to me at the time, that stranger's perspective gave me tremendous comfort and strength, one that

I shared with my siblings who greeted me at the train station in Providence.

Yes, he was still alive. I still had time to say that I loved him one more time. I still had time to tell him what a great dad he had always been. I still had time. The precious gift of time that I was now present to more than ever before. It was my wake-up call to just how precious each and every moment of life is.

We arrived at the hospital and went immediately to his room. He was attached to many life-saving devices. The room was so cold, but all I could see was his smile when he saw me enter the room. He was still alive. I still had time. Thank you God for giving me the gift of time to see my dad, perhaps, for the last time, to feel the warmth of his love in his smile and in his eyes.

Those precious moments changed me. They woke me up to living my life fully each day so that I have no regrets. We never know the time or place we will be called from this earth. I was lucky I got to be with my dad to see him smile, to say I loved him. And while he was never able to speak again, we were blessed with five more years of our dad being with us. During that time, our family shared many beautiful experiences, laughter and tears at his nursing home. Memories that will last a lifetime. We found joy even in the sadness that even though he was disabled, unable to walk or speak, he could still smile and hug us with his one good arm.

LIVING A LIFE WITH NO REGRETS

For many years, Bronnie Ware, a palliative care nurse had the privilege of being with patients the last weeks and moments of their lives. She said, "Never underestimate someone's capacity for growth in those last few weeks of life. They experience a wide gamut of emotions that range from denial, fear, anger, remorse, and, ultimately, acceptance. When asked if they would do anything differently if they had the opportunity to do it all over again, these were the common themes that surfaced.

5 COMMON REGRETS

1. I wish I hadn't worked so hard.

"Many regretted missing their children's youth and their partner's companionship because they spent too much time at the office and not enough time at home."

2. I wish I had let myself be happier.

"Many did not acknowledge that happiness was a choice. They stayed stuck in their old patterns of behavior. Fear of change and fear of stepping out of their comfort zone had them pretend they were happy when they actually longed to have more silliness and laughter in their lives.

"When you are on your deathbed, what others think of you is a long way from your mind. How wonderful it would be to let go, smile, and laugh again… Long before you are dying."

3. I wish I had the courage to express my feelings.

"Many people suppressed their feelings in order to keep peace with others. As a result, they settled for a mediocre existence and never became who they were truly capable of becoming.

Many developed illnesses related to bitterness, anger and resentment." While we can't control the actions of others, we can control how we respond. By speaking openly and honestly, we can impact the quality of relationships.

4. I wish I had the courage to live a life true to myself, not the lives others expected of me.

"This was the most common regret. When people realize their life is almost over and see their life more clearly, it is easy to see how many dreams went unfulfilled. Most people had not honored even half of their dreams and would die knowing it was choices they made or did not make."

5. I wish I had stayed in touch with my friends.

"Often, they would not realize the full benefit of old friends until their dying weeks and it was almost impossible to track them down. Many had become so caught up in their own lives that they let golden friendships slip over the years."

There were many regrets about not giving friendships the time and effort they deserved. It was not money or status that mattered to them; it all came down to love and relationships.

LESSONS LEARNED FROM THE DYING

Now is the time to take your life back and start living fully each day a life that has no regrets. It's time to wake up, to live intentionally every day for the rest of your life.

Perhaps, you have received a wake-up call of your own…

+ A frightening phone call.
+ A serious diagnosis.
+ A life-changing incident.

Each of these experiences are calls to action, motivating us to make a change. They are life's way of waking us up before it's too late. The question becomes, what will we do about it when we receive life's little or big reminders? Will we realize the time to change is now lest we live a life of regrets? If we are lucky enough to get a wake-up call, it is an opportunity for us to slow down, take stock of our lives, and make a course correction.

But sometimes our wake-up call is not as evident. It might manifest itself more subtly as an undercurrent of discontent with the way your life is going. Or it could show up as a yearning for something more and you are not clear about what more means.

- Allow yourself to become more aware of and acknowledge those churnings deep within.
- Become more conscious of what you are struggling with.

This pain, uncertainty, doubt, fear, anxiety, and overwhelming feeling can spark change and wake you up to the fact that:

- Maybe life doesn't have to continue going this way.
- Maybe you can reframe what your future looks like.
- Maybe you can take responsibility for the way your life is.
- Maybe you can disrupt those patterns that hold you back and harness them to attract the life of abundance that you deserve.

LIVE AS IF IT IS YOUR LAST DAY

People grow when faced with their own mortality. We are awakened to a life of purpose and passion, one that makes you jump out of bed in the morning.

- It is possible to fall in love with your own life all over again… or perhaps for the first time.
- It is possible to revitalize your excitement and drive when you live on purpose.

♦ It is possible to live our lives fully each day… as if it were our last.

FIVE WAYS TO LIVE WITHOUT REGRET

1. Spend quality time with your loved ones each day.
2. Live, laugh, love. Experience childlike curiosity and wonder each day.
3. Express what you were feeling. Courageously say what you want and what you don't want. Set boundaries.
4. Follow your own dreams, not someone else's.
5. Nurture friendships and relationships. Connect through meaningful conversations.

PERSPECTIVE

As we get a little older, we begin to gain perspective. In a recent article by Jenny Anderson of Inc. Magazine, Bill Gates reflected on his life. As a young man in his 20s, he was consumed with making Microsoft a personal computing giant.

Today, his focus is on other people.

"Did I devote enough time to my family?

Did I develop new friendships and deepen old ones?

At 25, these would have been laughable to me, but as I get older, they are much more meaningful."

The choices we make each day to be more connected to family, friends, and our community is what makes for a rich and abundant life. Love is the one true measure of a life well lived, and that is available to all of us. We must choose it and invest in it to reap the benefits. There is a tremendous cost to be paid when we live mediocre lives, when we do not fulfill our own dreams, when we put off investing in ourselves to be all we can be.

The biggest dream killers of all are statements like these:

+ I don't know how.
+ It's too late to try.
+ I will do it when...

It's not too late. Start where you are right now. You have all you need. Don't waste another minute. Focus on having more of what you do want and less of what you don't want in life.

Wake up. It's time for you to begin living the life you love. Do it now before it's too late

A PERSONAL REFLECTION

Two years ago, I chose to live a simpler life with less. It was one of the best decisions of my life. It was also when I began to realize that more of my life had passed than what was likely still ahead of me. As I started to reflect on my life, the lessons learned that shaped me into who I am, the highs and the lows, the joys and the sorrows, I became profoundly grateful and humbled for all that I have been given.

+ Loving parents and siblings, strong family values and work ethic.
+ Two amazing sons and daughters-in-law who taught me to love deeply.
+ Lifelong friends in a community of love and support.
+ A career that has provided endless opportunities to make a difference in the lives of others.
+ Peace and contentment that come with living a simpler, more abundant life with less.

◆ Having more time, more money, and more freedom to inspire and encourage others to consider living with less so they too can live more.

Life is a gift, one that is to be cherished. Having the opportunity to celebrate even one more day is one that I wholeheartedly embrace. I invite you to do the same. Live the life you love each and every day before it's too late.

The Wake-Up Assessment

Look at your life right now. Answer these questions fully and honestly. They will serve as an opportunity for you to face your own realities so you can make changes today that will allow you to live your life fully each day; one without regrets.

1. How are you spending quality time with your family and loved ones daily?

2. What areas of your life do you wish were better (i.e., relationship, family, finances, career, you time, personal, spiritual, and professional growth, health)

3. Do you allow yourself to be happy, content, and experience being in the moment? How could you slow down to allow for that in your life?

4. Do you clearly express your feelings or do you hide how you really feel?

5. Are you living true to your own values or those of others around you?

6. Do you maintain and nurture your relationships or are you waiting for them to contact and connect with you?

CHAPTER EIGHT

Downsize and Downsize by Decluttering

Thirty-four years ago, Bob and Karen bought a house in a great neighborhood that was filled with many other young families. It was within walking distance of schools, church, and ball fields. It was within a reasonable commute to work for both of them. They raised their children in that house. Their well-worn kitchen table hosted hundreds of family dinners, multiple birthday parties, science projects, craft activities, homework sessions and lively conversations.

A few months ago, after many long discussions, Bob and Karen finally decided to sell their family home and downsize to a smaller, one-story house closer to where their children and grandchildren live. It was time. They spent months talking about the kind of lifestyle they wanted now that they were both retired. They looked at numerous lifestyle communities that were close to their daughters' homes. They did their due diligence with regard to affordability, walkability, and proximity not just to their children and grandchildren but also to retail stores, doctors, and cultural activities that they enjoy. They asked many questions along the way.

They finally decided that the timing was right for them to say goodbye to the home they raised their children in. It was time for them to downsize and declutter so they would have more time to pursue what mattered most to them - being near to their family, being able to participate in their children's and grandchildren's lives while they are still young and healthy enough. They would also live close enough that their children would be able to assist them as they age.

Bob and Karen were finally ready to make new memories, to make a dramatic lifestyle change because they had a clear vision for what mattered most to them. Their decision to downsize was not an easy one to make, but they realized that the short-term pain they would experience would be well worth the long-term gain of living closer to their family and loved ones. It took time and an incredible amount of fortitude and physical effort. It was emotional and not without tears. But today, they are living their dream, making new memories and many new friends. The last time I saw them, they were at a soccer game cheering for their young grandson.

If you are asking yourself any of these questions, you are not alone.

- What are the benefits of downsizing?
- Is there a downside to downsizing?
- How do I know when it is the right time to downsize?
- What kind of lifestyle do I want/ where do I want to live?
- Is there an easy way to downsize?

The decision to downsize and/or declutter is on the mind of many Americans. The Minimalist Movement, or at least the appeal of living a simpler, less cluttered life is having a profound impact on the American mindset and culture. It has been a wake-up call to those of us who have spent over half of our lives accumulating more... when the secret to real happiness and freedom can actually be found in needing and wanting less.

When major life changes occur, either expectedly or unexpectedly, we might have no choice but to downsize. Divorce, serious health or financial crisis, or death of a spouse or loved one are just a few of the circumstances that might force the decision to downsize. But it is when you do have the opportunity to choose to downsize to a smaller home or live with less that the thought of such a monumental lifestyle change can be completely overwhelming. In fact, it is at this point that many people get stopped and don't even try because they are confronted by the unknown and overwrought with what it would take to disrupt their current lifestyle and circumstances.

- ◆ "What if I don't like my new home or my new lifestyle?"
- ◆ "What if I miss my old friends, neighbors, and neighborhood?"

Of course, like anything else in life, you probably won't know unless you try. Making the wrong decision can be an expensive mistake that none of us want to make. That is why I encourage you to take your time, consider various options, do your homework and due diligence before making any decision that will change your life. But if you are the least bit curious, if you are exploring the idea of downsizing, or if you are wondering if you should stay or you should go, then keep reading. Slow down. Notice your current quality of life: relationships, business, health, work/life balance.

Begin to ask yourself the following questions:

- What difference will downsizing make in your life?
- Why do you want to downsize, declutter, and live with less?
- What do you want and need to make more room for in your life that you don't have now?
- What is your vision for a simpler, more fulfilling and meaningful life?

Know Why You Want to Downsize

The first and most important question you need to ask yourself is… Why do I want to downsize? This will be the motivation that anchors you in the midst of change and transition, helping you to succeed with the downsizing process.

- Bob and Karen knew their why. They wanted to live closer to their children and grandchildren so they could participate in each other's lives more fully.
- I knew my why. I wanted a simpler life with less so I could have more time, money, and freedom to pursue what mattered most to me.
- What is your why?

What Are the Upsides of Downsizing?
The 5 top benefits of downsizing:

1. More time. Less stuff.

Getting rid of excess possessions and clutter helps you to make room for what matters most to you. When you have more time, money, and freedom, you free up your lifestyle and have the opportunity to experience your life more fully. Living in a smaller space with less stuff, fewer possessions, and fewer distractions contribute to a higher quality of life. Smaller homes enable families to spend more quality time together, often leading to a happier home.

2. More freedom. Less expense.

With a smaller house and property to furnish, maintain, clean, manage, and pay for, there is more opportunity to save and invest your money and resources on what matters most for your new lifestyle (i.e., travel, education, experiences). Downsizing can be a first step to streamlining and taking back control of your life. Rather than resenting your big home and all that it entails, begin to love your new small home and the opportunities that living with less provides.

3. More peace of mind. Less stress.

Too much stuff contributes to stress, anxiety, and the feeling of being overwhelmed. Owning less and having to care for less provides peace of mind and a better quality of life. Downsizing helps you prioritize your life, bringing into your home only what is necessary and contributes to your happiness.

4. More mobility and flexibility. Less responsibility.

Time and freedom are precious commodities that become more available when we own less and live with less. We have the opportunity to become more agile and mobile when we own and have to care for less. Downsizing can be the beginning of a new chapter, a fresh start and focus on what matters most to you.

5. More efficiency. Less waste.

A good floor plan will work harder to accommodate the demands of your new lifestyle. Great design begins with great function. When your new home is highly functional and efficient for your unique lifestyle needs, you waste less time, energy, and resources. It impacts the quality of how you will live, work, and entertain.

What if I can't afford to move or if I'm not ready yet? Downsize by decluttering

The reality is that not everyone can afford to move or they may not be ready to move. Yet, they still want to live a less cluttered life. This actually provides a great opportunity to anyone at any time to **downsize by decluttering**. It does not necessitate a move, but it does reap many of the same upside benefits of downsizing that contribute to a simpler, richer life with less.

Downsizing by decluttering has become a very popular choice for people at every age, particularly for baby boomers who have spent a lifetime buying more. For whatever reason, and there are many, we have accumulated a lot. Our houses, attics, garages, basements, cupboards and closets, and even our storage units are overflowing with way too much stuff. The average American home has over 300,000 items in it, according to a study by the University of California.

All of this stuff contributes to stress, anxiety, and less time for what matters to us. The irony is that we work hard to earn money so we can buy more and continue to overwhelm ourselves with more than we want, need, or if we are truthful, even wish for.

If this resonates you, there are several small actions you can take to alleviate some of the stress and the overwhelming feeling so you will start to see immediate results.

5 Steps to Downsize by Decluttering

1. Stop buying more.

As obvious as this might seem, if you want to live a simpler less cluttered life, you need to first stop buying more. You sabotage your own efforts when you continue to add more into your life.

2. Start by paying attention to how much you already have.

Take time to look around to see how much you currently own. Also observe how much you have that you don't use (i.e. clothes, shoes, kitchen utensils).

3. Practice discerning what you actually need vs. what you think you want.

Will one more pair of awesome boots add to the quality of your simpler life or will they detract from it? When you are tempted to buy something new, simply ask yourself if you actually need it and how it will add value to your simpler lifestyle.

4. Make a habit of using what you have and buying only what you need.

Try getting creative with what you can make for dinner using what you have or try accessorizing clothes you already own. Challenge yourself to "make due." Surprise yourself with how much time and money you can save.

5. Start the editing process today.

Don't wait. Look around your house. Walk through each room. What do you no longer want, need or use? Immediately begin removing them from your house (dispose, donate or sell). Get rid of any duplicates or triplicates (pantry items, kitchen utensils).

Notice how much excess you have accumulated. As you begin to see results, build on the momentum. Also involve your family and friends in the process. Most of all, try to make it fun.

These are just a few actions you can take immediately to downsize by decluttering your home, office, car... your life. As you begin to move toward a less cluttered, more intentional life, you will experience more peace of mind, more time to enjoy what matters most to you, and freedom to focus on the life you really want.

Are there downsides to downsizing?

As with any big decision, it is important to weigh the pros and cons of downsizing too. These are a few downsides to downsizing that you should consider:

1. Downsizing is an emotional experience.

One of the main reasons people choose to stay in their homes is that they are reluctant to face the emotional aspect of downsizing their home and their possessions. Your head may be telling you downsizing is a smart idea, but your heart might be telling you something else. You have many memories of experiences, so it is sad to think of leaving all of that behind, but memories remain and you can create new memories wherever you live. While you might not always acknowledge your attachment to your stuff, there will likely be moments when your emotions and memories will be triggered. During the process of my own downsizing journey, I was reduced to tears on numerous occasions:

- My dad's alarm clock triggered sweet memories of him waking up early to provide for our family.

- My mom's silver Christmas garland that graced every mantle of every home we lived in.
- My son, Kevin's macaroni picture frame that he made with love for a Mother's Day gift.
- My son, Sean's handwritten note he gave to me as he went off to college.

Rather than holding on to those tangible mementoes, I taught myself to take photos of them and then let them go. I created a Shutterfly album with stories about each memory so that one day when I am no longer here, my family will know just how much those little things meant to me. If you are not willing to let go, downsizing may not be for you.

2. Downsizing means saying goodbye and letting go.

Downsizing is a process. It takes time to let go. When you have a clear vision of the new lifestyle you want, and when you begin moving toward it, you will begin to see that the sacrifice you make today will make room for the new lifestyle you want tomorrow.

3. Downsizing reality number one.

When you downsize or right-size, you will likely have less space, so you will need to dispose of, donate or give away precious heirlooms you might have been holding onto for a long time. The reality is that your loved ones may not need or want those precious heirlooms that you have been saving for them. Learning to let go and detach from your possessions is a muscle and a mindset that you can develop with practice. It becomes easier and less emotional over time.

4. Downsizing means you will have less living space, work space, and storage space.

Decisions need to be made about what fits and what doesn't fit in your new smaller space. You will need to discover new ways to live, work, and entertain. You will need to find furniture and storage that serve more than one purpose.

5. Downsizing can be expensive.

The cost of moving can be expensive. Before downsizing, first know the costs related to selling your home, moving, buying or renting. Many people overestimate what their current home is worth and underestimate what a new home will cost. There are also intangible costs that should be considered. You will miss old friends, convenient stores, and doctors, but you will also find new ones.

6. Downsizing means making tough decisions

If you take too much stuff with you, you will probably overcrowd your new smaller space, forcing you to go through the process again (double downsizing) or you will have to incur the wasted additional expense of a storage unit, which defeats the purpose of learning to live with less.

7. Downsizing will turn your world upside down for a period of time.

Leaving the house you raised your children in is disruptive enough, but you are also leaving old friends, neighbors, and other favorite things. You are moving from the comfortable and familiar to the uncomfortable and new. Expect your life to be disrupted for a period of time. Also, expect that it will all be worth it in the end.

How do you know if and when it's the right time to downsize or right-size?

As we approach new seasons of our lives, we are faced with new opportunities, challenges, and decisions that need to be made. This is especially true of baby boomers who might be thinking about or are nearing retirement. The possibility of creating a whole new lifestyle in this next chapter can be exciting, and at the same time, confronting and stressful. Many home owners have begun to realize that "living large" doesn't necessarily mean that bigger is better.

Should I stay or should I go?

Perhaps, one of the most demanding decisions we might face is whether we should remain in our existing home or search for a new living situation that will better suit our current lifestyle, while also anticipating what future needs we might encounter as we age. While there is no way to predict what that future might hold for us, the question becomes, "How do we know if and when it is the right time to downsize?"

To help discern if and when you should downsize, there are several important questions you might begin to ask yourself:

1. Assess your current home and living situation.

A. Affordability

Is your home "comfortably affordable?" According to a Harvard study, approximately 39 million Americans can't afford the home they live in and approximately 19 million are spending over 50% of their income on housing.

If you are spending more than you can reasonably afford, it might be time to reevaluate the affordability of your home, or else risk compromising your overall financial health. It might be time to find a less expensive place to live, one that provides comfortability and financial peace of mind, putting more money in your pocket while also having a life.

B. Livability

What does livability mean? It is the degree to which a space (home or community) is suitable or right to live in, to satisfy your wants and needs at a particular time in your life. It is age-appropriate for a particular time of your life. It impacts the quality of your life and how well you will live, work, and play… your happiness and overall wellbeing.

Perhaps, this is one reason why, according to AARP, 90% of Americans would prefer to stay in their home as they age. It is comfortable and carries a lifetime of memories. It might be in a great neighborhood that is close to family and friends. At one point in your life, your home was perfect for raising a family. It was near schools, work, grocery stores, parks, and recreation. It was perfect for two or three kids, two or three cars, and a busy family. No wonder we want to hold onto that time of our lives and those precious memories. No wonder it's hard to let go of a home that was once a perfect fit for that period of our lives.

But is it the right choice for your lifestyle right now?

- Do you have **unused spaces** that you are paying to heat, cool, and maintain?
  - If your kids are grown and now living on their own, do you really need those two or three extra bedrooms and baths?
  - How well are you utilizing your basement, attic, and garage? Are they storing boxes of stuff you haven't seen or used in years? Are you holding onto precious heirlooms to give your kids someday... even though they may not even want them?

- Do you have **underutilized spaces** that you rarely use or no longer need?
  - Notice how many of your rooms you actually use each day, each week, each year (living room, dining room, extra bathrooms, guest room, etc.).
  - Notice how much it is costing you to pay for the underutilized real estate in your home for the limited number of times you actually use them each year? As an interior designer for many years, I help my clients see those spaces differently so they can make sense of them as their life needs change.

In an attempt to weigh costs of staying or moving and to discern if your house will be a good fit for you as you age, rethink ways you can repurpose unused or underutilized space in your home, making it worthwhile and cost effective to remain in your current home. On the other hand, you might discover that the big house is too much for you and that it might be time to downsize or right-size to a home that better suits your current needs, as well as your future needs.

C. Navigability and accessibility

Are there areas of your home that are becoming less navigable and accessible for you?

Will your two or three-story home still be suitable for you when you are older?

Will your soaking tub or tub/ shower still be safe and easy for you to get in and out of in the future as mobility becomes an issue?

Perhaps, like many Americans, you want to stay in your home for as long as possible as you age. Aging in Place renovations make it possible for you to live independently longer by:

- Making your home easier and safer to live in as you age
- Giving you the ability to continue accessing all areas of your home

Aging in Place addresses many issues to accommodate mobility and accessibility. These are just a few:

- Grab bars
- Chair lifts or elevators
- Ramps or sloped walkways
- No step entryways
- Walk-in showers with no threshold
- Raised toilets

- Non-slip flooring
- Call systems and security
- Wider doorways and hallways
- Lever hardware
- Adjustments to kitchen and bath counter heights
- First-floor bedrooms and baths
- Upgraded lighting

The costs to remodel for Aging in Place can vary widely from the most basic and necessary retrofits (lever hardware, faucets, grab bars and lighting) to the most extensive and expansive renovations. Those large renovations often include first-floor master bedroom/ master bathroom suites, elevators, wider hallways and doorways, and full kitchen renovations.

After assessing your current home and living situation for **affordability, livability, navigability,** and accessibility, the next area to look is the season of life that you are in.

2. Assess your current life season, life stage, and life circumstance.

A. Your life season.

It is certainly important to understand how life's stages impact how we think, plan and decide on what's next in our lives, but it is equally important to listen to our life season that motivates our desire for change. When we begin to notice what we long for or what we are discontent about in our lives, it becomes apparent that we might be ready to take a chance, get out of our comfort zone and make the necessary changes that will allow us to live a more fulfilled life in the next season of our life.

Notice if you hear yourself saying…

It's time…
- To let go of (this house, memories, etc.) so I can move on with my life.
- For us. Our kids are grown, so we want more time to travel, explore, etc.

It makes sense…
- To downsize to a smaller more manageable home or apartment.
- To save money on a smaller more affordable home; money we could use for travel or a more comfortable retirement.

I'm ready for…
- A simpler life with less.
- A new chapter, a new challenge.
- Change (even though I'm not sure what that is yet).

I want…
- To enjoy my life more, to have more time and money to travel more while I'm still healthy and active.
- To live closer to my kids and grandkids.

I don't want…
- To live here anymore. We've outgrown the house and neighborhood.
- To age alone.

As we leave an old season and enter a new season of our lives, we will often hear those "little voices" that are calling us to change. By paying attention to those inner longing or areas of discontent, we begin to understand what is motivating our desire for change.

+ Joanna had been widowed for 4 years. After Tom's death she made a decision to stay in the home they lived in together for over 20 years. She thought it would help her heal, but recently she heard herself saying, "I know I have to let go of this house and memories because it's holding me back from building a new life for myself."

  She started noticing a desire for change. It may take a while for her to make the move, but the act of listening to her inner voice may be what motivates her to let go of the past so she can start living her own new life in the future.

+ Christine, a corporate executive, has traveled all over the world on business for the last 25 years. As much as she has loved her prestigious and challenging career, lately, she has heard herself saying, "I don't want to do this anymore. I want something more, something more fulfilling, but I'm not sure what that is."

  She began noticing how much she enjoyed and missed time with her family and friends. She began noticing that getting on planes to exotic destinations was no longer exciting to her. She felt herself longing for a simpler, less stressful life filled with more time for herself, her family, and friends.

By paying attention to what matters most, Christine is excited to be retiring in a few months and discovering a life that is more meaningful and gratifying.

Begin to listen to your own inner yearning and feelings of discontent. They will help you discern your own life season and what you want, and what might be the best choice for your next stage of life.

B. Assess your life stage.

In addition to understanding how your *life season* impacts your motivation and desire for change, your *life stage* plays a key role in your decision-making process.

Empty Nest.

Kids are launched. You have done your best to prepare them to handle life's challenges on their own. After the initial emotions adjustment and sense of sadness and loss, after wondering what to do with the extra bedroom, you might even find yourself wondering what to do with your extra time. The transition to full-time parenting and a full house to an empty nest is an eventuality that all parents face with mixed emotion. But it is also a time to experience your newfound time and freedom, something you haven't had for many years. It is a time to reconnect with your spouse and with yourself. It is a time to rediscover hobbies and interests that were put on the back burner and explore your bucket list with a new sense of excitement and possibility.

This is also the time you might begin to realize that your house is just too big and you have outgrown your old neighborhood. You might even begin to consider different housing and lifestyle options you never thought of for yourself before. City living?

International lifestyle? Fifty-five plus community? Perhaps, for the first time, you are exploring options that would better suit your new carefree lifestyle, in which case, you realize that downsizing to a smaller space while you are still healthy and active might be the right choice for you. On the other hand, you might decide that you still love your big family home, your neighbors, and neighborhood, so you might decide to stay and age in place for as long as you can.

Whatever you decide, the empty nest stage of life challenges and inspires you to think differently about whether you should stay or whether you should go. This process takes time to think about and to decide what the right choice will be for you in your new child-free lifestyle. It's part of life's exciting new journey.

Retirement.

Retirement as our parents once knew it no longer exist in America. Baby boomers have been reinventing retirement. We are choosing to work longer, create new businesses, or go back to school. We are healthier and more active than our parents' generation. We are young at heart and do what we can to look younger, stay in shape, and on some level we are refusing to grow old. Our desire to live longer and healthier lives in retirement is reflected in the mindset of many baby boomers who want to be defined by their attitude, not by their age.

"I still have so much more that I want to do and accomplish. I am doing my best to live life to the fullest each day in retirement, and I'm doing it my way."

The transition from full-time employment to working less and having more free time is a turning point that provides more freedom and new choices, including where and how we will live in retirement.

Retirement trends suggest that baby boomers prefer to live in walkable communities with age-appropriate housing options. They want easy access to public transportation, health care, restaurants, entertainment, culture, education, and shopping. Safety, security and affordability are also extremely important to baby boomers. These types of supportive communities and environments help baby boomers balance work and play, impacting the quality of their life and independent lifestyle. At this stage, their focus is on being comfortable, active, and enjoying their lifestyle, where they can embrace their new identity and thrive.

Elderhood

Aging is inevitable. It happens to all of us whether we embrace it or not. With aging comes the more obvious signs—gray hair, wrinkles, senior moments, and the normal aches and pains. As much as we might want to deny the aging process, if we are lucky enough to age into our eighties and nineties, there is a strong likelihood that we will need some form of physical assistance to continue a higher quality of life.

And with an ever-increasing number of older adults who are living longer and wanting to age well as much as possible, there is a strong movement to live with less by living in communities that provide not only for age-related changes but also shared social interaction and responsibilities.

By assessing your life stage, you can better discern what might be the best choice of where and how you live as you begin to need more assistance.

C. Assess your life circumstances.

Divorce, death of a spouse or loved one, health, emergency or financial crisis.

Each of these significant life-changing events suddenly alters our perspective and changes our priorities. They force us to make lifestyle decisions based on our new expected or unexpected life circumstances. These life changes make us adapt and pivot. Our choices will likely be more limited than they once were.

- As a new caregiver, you might not have a choice but to modify your home to accommodate an aging parent who can no longer live safely alone.
- As a new divorcee or widow, you might now choose to live closer to supportive and nurturing family and friends in an environment where you can begin to heal.
- As someone who is facing a financial crisis, you might not have a choice but to downsize to a smaller, affordable living situation to reduce expenses and, perhaps, even share expenses.

These life circumstances challenge us to think differently. They drive our lifestyle decisions based on our new reality—sometimes with little or no time to plan at all.

DOWNSIZING, SIMPLE, EASY, FUN?

If I knew that downsizing would change my life, would I do it again? Would I have done it sooner? Absolutely! Or if I had been really smart, I never would have accumulated so much in the first place. The first day of my downsizing journey started on January 1, 2016. Tears streaming down my face, I looked up and cried. "How will I ever downsize this much stuff? How can I possibly manage such a large project by myself, which will be so physically and emotionally exhausting?"

It was larger than any project I'd ever taken on personally. Little did I know that it would change my life. If you were to ask me if I was ever overwhelmed, stuck or just wanted to quit, I would answer with a resounding yes! And add… at least 100 times to that statement. But I am ever grateful for persevering to the end. Thanks to my dear family and friends, I made it to the finish line.

The great news is that I learned so much about downsizing while downsizing. In fact, I created a design process that benefited me and one that I can now share with you that will help make your downsizing journey simple, efficient, and fun. I call it the ABCs of Downsizing because these 3 simple steps will help you visualize your way to success. I also created a video on YouTube explaining how it works. https://www.youtube.com/watch?v=VTwvspn30RI&t=1s

HOW TO MAKE DOWNSIZING SIMPLE, EFFICIENT, AND FUN

Can downsizing really be that simple and fun? The answer is yes when you follow these 3 simple steps that will create strong visuals for you as you plan your own downsizing journey.

The 3 simple steps are:

1. Create your own ABC List.
2. Create a spreadsheet that inventories your ABC List.
3. Create a dimensioned furniture floor plan of your new space.

Creating your own ABC list will help you get organized and get real about what you need and want…or don't need and don't want. Keep your vision alive. Stay focused on why you want to downsize and live a simpler life with less.

Walk through your home with 3 colors of large post-it notes.

Tag each A item: These are items that you just can't live without. They will be going with you to your new home. Consolidate all A items into one area of each room.

Tag each C item: Give them to family or friends. Sell or donate. Have all C items removed from your house immediately and you will already begin to see progress.

That leaves you with the B items: These are more difficult to distinguish and may eventually end up being moved to the A or C list as you continue the process.

2. CREATE A SPREADSHEET THAT INVENTORIES YOUR ABC LIST

Room by Room, inventory, photo, and measure all existing furniture, lamps, art, and accessories.

Insert into ABC spreadsheet. This spreadsheet will assist you with keeping track of where each item will be going.

3. CREATE A FURNITURE FLOOR PLAN
(Or hire a professional interior designer to help you)

Measure your new space. Create a dimensioned CAD drawing of each new room.

Plot in all A items. Plot in B items as the space allows. Once you have created a furniture floor plan utilizing as many of your A items and B items as possible, it will become apparent that based on the size and layout of your new home not all A and B items will fit, so you will have to rethink which items will work and look best in your new home. Sell, donate, or give away the unused B items.

Edit your ABC list as needed and rework your furniture floor plan. There is no point in putting too much into your new space only to have to downsize once again soon after you move in. Once you have a final floor plan, you may need to purchase some furniture that is either of smaller scale or multifunctional. If it doesn't fit, don't bring it with you.

Why have an ABC list?

Your furniture floor plan will make your move easier, faster, and more efficiently. You will feel confident that the furniture you are bringing will be properly scaled to your new smaller space. You won't be bringing items you don't need—things that will only clutter your new home.

Other Downsizing Tips

* Build a team. Engage your family and friends in the process.
* Schedule work in 3-4 hour increments.
* Work on 1 small area of your home at a time.
* Remove all C items from your home immediately. Don't look back.
* Create a small box in each room for emotional items that can be dealt with on another day. This is intended to not slow the process.

BONUS: 58 places to donate your stuff to a good cause

People are always asking me where to donate their stuff. I've compiled a list that I've used myself. I hope that it's helpful to you.

GENERAL HOUSEHOLD ITEMS:

1. ENCORE SHOP: https://www.chestercountyhospital.org/giving/get-involved/shop-with-purpose/the-encore-shop
What they do: Our philosophy is to offer quality merchandise for resale. What they need: Clothing, furniture, jewelry.

2. MINISTRY OF CARING: https://www.ministryofcaring.org/
What they do: a vibrant community of staff, volunteers, donors, and diverse supporters united by a passion to serve the poor.

What they need: new or lightly used clothing for the poor is always appreciated. So are new toilet articles and other household items and furniture in good condition.

3. GOODWILL: http://www.goodwill.org/
What they do: Help people with barriers to employment learn skills to find competitive employment.

What they need: Clothing, electronics, appliances, furniture and more.

4. SALVATION ARMY: https://www.salvationarmyusa.org/usn/
What they do: Provide community programs, homeless services, rehabilitation, disaster relief and other assistance to those in need.
What they need: Clothing, furniture, household goods, sporting equipment, books, electronics, and more.

5. VIETNAM VETERANS OF AMERICA: https://vva.org/
What they do: Help Vietnam-era veterans and their families.

What they need: clothing, baby items, housewares, electronics, small appliances, tools and just about anything else.

6. VOLUNTEERS OF AMERICA: https://www.voa.org/
What they do: Support at-risk youth, the frail elderly, men and women returning from prison, homeless individuals and families, people with disabilities, and those recovering from addictions.

What they need: clothing, furniture toys, and household goods for their thrift stores.

7. CAUSE USA: https://cause-usa.org/
What they do: Send gift packs to wounded military personnel and their families.

What they need: Playing cards, handheld electronic games, current magazines, batteries, travel-size toiletries, and more.

CLOTHING, SHOES, AND ACCESSORIES:

8. DELAWARE BREAST CANCER COALITION | GREAT STUFF SAVVY RESALE: http://greatstuffresale.com/
What they do: The shop offers a variety of high-quality items, including women's clothing, shoes, and jewelry. We also have a section for designer clothing, evening wear, business attire, and petites.

What they need: High-quality women's clothing, shoes, accessories, furniture and decorative items.

9. BEEBE'S TREASURE CHEST THRIFT SHOP: https://www.beebehealthcare.org/make-gift/thrift-shop
What they do: a fundraising success for Beebe Healthcare, aiding

the Beebe Auxiliary in its tireless effort to support the healthcare that it brings to the community.

What they need: Men, women, and children's clothing.

10. DESIGNERS CONSIGNER:
http://designerconsignerde.com/
What they do: Delaware's premier upscale resale boutique, packed full of all the brands you want, at reasonable prices!

What they need: Upscale designer clothing and accessories for men and women.

11. SUITING WARRIORS: https://suitingwarriors.org/
What they do: provides transitioning assistance to the men and women of the U.S. Armed Forces, Veterans, their spouses, Guard and Reserve by providing them with upscale professional attire needed to compete in the civilian workforce.

What they need: New or gently-used men's and women's professional attire.

12. DRESS FOR SUCCES: https://dressforsuccess.org/
What they do: Provide interview skills, confidence boosts, and career development to low-income women in over 75 cities worldwide.

What they need: Women's business suits and other professional apparel, footwear, and accessories.

13. CAREER GEAR: https://careergear.org/
What they do: Provide underserved job-seeking men with training, career counseling, interviews, and professional clothing.
What they need: Men's suits, dress shirts, ties, shoes, briefcases, and other interview-appropriate clothing.

14. SEW MUCH COMFORT:

http://www.sewmuchcomfort.org/

What they do: Provide adaptive clothing to wounded service men and women in military hospitals (specially designed to look like normal attire while accommodating their injuries).

What they need: Basketball shorts, boxers, t-shirts, sweatshirts, and PJ bottom, as well as twill, flannel, and woven shirt fabric.

15. PLANET AID: http://www.planetaid.org/

What they do: Provide clothing to people in developing nations and fund community, health, agricultural, and vocational programs.

What they need: gently-used, unsoiled, functional clothing and shoes.

16. SOLES FOR SOULS: https://soles4souls.org/

What they do: Distribute shoes to people in need in over 125 countries.

What they need: All types of new or gently-worn shoes: athletic, running, dress, sandals, pumps, heels, work boots, cleats, dance and flip flops.

WEDDING AND PROM DRESSES:

17. BRIDES AGAINST BREAST CANCER:

https://www.bridesagainstbreastcancer.org/

What they do: Advance the awareness of breast cancer and operate a wish-granting service, enabling patients to make special memories with their loved ones.

What they need: new and used wedding gowns from 2005 to present.

18. BRIDES ACROSS AMERICA:

https://www.bridesacrossamerica.com/

What they do: Provide wedding gowns to military brides in need.

What they need: New or gently-used bridal gowns not more than three years old.

19. GLASS SLIPPER PROJECT:

https://www.glassslipperproject.org/

What they do: Collect formal dresses and accessories and provide them, free of charge, to students who are unable to purchase their own prom attire.

What they need: New and almost-new prom dresses and accessories.

BABY AND CHILDREN'S ITEMS:

20. PROJECT NIGHT NIGHT:

http://www.projectnightnight.org/

What they do: Reduce the trauma of homeless children with Night Night Packages or childhood comforts.

What they need: stuffed animals, blankets, and children's books.

21. SAFE (STUFFED ANIMALS FOR EMERGENCIES):

https://stuffedanimalsforemergencies.org/

What they do: collect items to give to children in emotional, traumatic, or stressful situations (like fires, illness, abuse, homelessness, and natural disasters).

What they need: New or gently-used stuffed animals.

22. PROJECT SMILE: http://www.projectsmile.org/
What they do: Provide emergency responders with children's comfort items to help ease their pain and fear.

What they need: New or gently-used stuffed animals, children's books, unused coloring books, new crayons.

23. NEWBORNS IN NEED: https://newbornsinneed.org/
What they do: Provide care necessities to local agencies and hospitals serving premature, ill, or impoverished newborns.

What they need: Baby clothing, toys, and other items, as well as fabric, yarn, thread, and other supplies.

24. RONALD MCDONALD HOUSE:
https://www.rmhc.org/
What they do: Provide a "home-away-from-home" for families so they can stay close by their hospitalized child at little or no cost.

What they need: New toys, food, and household products.

ELECTRONICS:

25. WORLD COMPUTER EXCHANGE:
https://worldcomputerexchange.org/
What they do: Provide used computers and technology to schools, libraries, community centers, and universities.

What they need: Computers, laptops, printers, hard drives, software and more.

26. NATIONAL CHRISTINA FOUNDATION:
http://www.ncadv.org/
What they do: Work to eliminate domestic violence and empower battered women and children.

What they need: Used cell phones.

27. COMPUTER RECYCLING CENTER:

https://its.temple.edu/lab/computer-recycling-center
What they do: Place computer in public charity and community programs through Computers & Education,™ and recycle unusable items to keep them out of landfills.

What they need: Computers, laptops, home electronics.

28. CELLPHONES FOR SOLDIERS:

https://www.cellphonesforsoldiers.com/
What they do: Use the money from recycling cell phones to purchase calling cards for troops in need.

What they need: used cell phones.

OFFICE AND SCHOOL SUPPLIES:

29. MUSCULAR DYSTROPHY FOUNDATION:

https://www.mda.org/
What they do: Fund worldwide research efforts and nationwide programs to aid with neuromuscular diseases and their families.

What they need: Computers, software, office equipment, furniture, and supplies for use in local offices.

30. DEVELOP AFRICA: https://www.developafrica.org/
What they do: Provide books, schools and teaching supplies, scholarships, and job-related training in Africa.

What they need: A wide variety of school and office supplies.

BOOKS:

31. INTERNATIONAL BOOK PROJECT:

https://www.intlbookproject.org/

What they do: Promote education and literacy by sending quality used books overseas.

What they need: Textbooks, dictionaries, encyclopedias, vocational books, children's books and more.

32. BOOKS FOR AFRICA: https://www.booksforafrica.org/

What they do: Help create a culture of literacy by shipping books to libraries and classrooms in Africa.

What they need: A wide variety of new and gently-used books.

33. THE BRIDGE OF BOOKS FOUNDATION:

https://bridgeofbooksfoundation.org/

What they do: Provide books to children in low-income families, particularly through foster family agencies, homeless shelters, underfunded schools, and neighborhood centers.

What they need: new and used children's books, from preschool through high school.

34. BOOKS THROUGH BARS:

http://booksthroughbars.org/

What they do: Send quality reading and educational material to prisoners, thereby promoting successful community re-integration.

What they need: A variety of new and gently-used books. Please email them before shipping.

35. BOOKS FOR SOLDIERS: http://booksforsoldiers.com/
What they do: Facilitate the direct donation of books to soldiers serving overseas.

What they need: Books and magazines (as well as CDs, DVDs, and video games) requested by soldiers.

DVDs AND CDs:

36. KID FLICKS: http://www.kidflicks.org/
What they do: Create movie libraries for children's hospitals and pediatric wards across the U.S.

What they need: DVDs.

37. MUSICIANS ON CALL:
https://www.musiciansoncall.org/
What they do: Provide hospitals with complete CD libraries and players for patient use.

What they need: New or gently-used CDs and new/ unused personal CD players.

ART AND CRAFT SUPPLIES:

38. BINKY PATROL: https://binkypatrol.org/
What they do: Distribute homemade blankets (sewn, knitted, crocheted, or quilted) to children in need.

What they need: Fabric, yarn, batting and finished blankets.

39. MANY ARMS REACH YOU: http://www.manyarms.org/
What they do: Collect and donate knitted, quilted or crocheted blankets to disadvantaged mothers and their children.

What they need: Yarn.

40. THE MOTHER BEAR PROJECT:

http://motherbearproject.org/

What they do: Provide hand-knit and crocheted bears to children with HIV/ AIDS in emerging nations.

What they need: Yarn, knitting needles, PolyFill, postage stamps, and packing tape.

41. KNOTS OF LOVE: http://www.knotsoflove.org/

What they do: Provide crocheted and knitted caps for chemo patients and others facing life-threatening illnesses and injuries.

What they need: Yarn.

42. MADE 4 AID: http://www.made4aid.org/

What they do: Sell handmade items on Etsy to raise funds for Doctors Without Borders.

What they need: A variety of handmade items, as well as arts and crafts material.

SPORTS EQUIPMENT:

43. SPORTS GIFT: http://www.sportsgift.org/

What they do: Provide sports programs and equipment to impoverished and disadvantaged children throughout the world.

What they need: A wide variety of sports equipment.

44. ONE WORLD RUNNING:

http://oneworldrunning.com/

What they do: provide running shoes to those in need in the US and throughout the world.

What they need: New and near-new running shoes.

45. BIKES FOR THE WORLD:

https://www.bikesfortheworld.org/

What they do: Donate bicycles to developing countries so that individuals can get to work or school, or provide health and education services to low-income rural people.

What they need: Any serviceable adult or children's bicycles, as well as bike parts, tools and accessories.

46. BICYCLES FOR HUMANITY:

http://bicycles-for-humanity.org/

What they do: Send bicycles to developing countries to empower disadvantaged people through improved access to food and water, employment, healthcare, education, and social opportunities.

What they need: bicycles, as well as, bike parts, tools, clothing, helmets, tires, and tubes.

47. PEACE PASSERS: http://peacepassers.org/

What they do: Distribute soccer supplies to communities in need to empower the youth and maximize hope.

What they need: soccer gear like balls, shoes, jerseys, shorts, and socks.

MUSICAL INSTRUMENTS:

48. MR. HOLLAND'S OPUS FOUNDATION:

https://www.mhopus.org/

What they do: Keep music alive in our schools and communities by donating musical instruments, under-Gently-used band or orchestral instruments.

49. EDUCATION THROUGH MUSIC:

https://etmonline.org/
What they do: Promote the integration of music into the curricula of disadvantaged schools in order to enhance students' academic performance and general development.

What they need: A variety of musical instruments.

EYEGLASSES:

50. UNITE FOR SIGHT: https://www.uniteforsight.org/
What they do: Support eye care for patients living in extreme poverty in developing countries.

What they need: new reading glasses, distance glasses, and sunglasses.

51. ONE SIGHT: https://onesight.org/
What they do: Provide free vision care and eyewear to people in need around the world. What they need: Gently-used eyewear.

52. NEW EYES FOR THE NEEDY:
https://www.new-eyes.org/
What they do: Send eyeglasses to medical missions and international charitable organizations for distribution to the poor in developing nations.

What they need: Eyeglasses, reading glasses, sunglasses, and hearing aids.

CARS:

53. BIG BROTHERS BIG SISTERS CARS FOR KIDS SAKE:
https://www.bbbs.org/cars-for-kids-sake/
What they do: Provide children facing adversity with strong and enduring, professionally supported one-to-one relationships that change their lives for the better.

What they need: All types of vehicles, including cars, trucks, SUVs, motor homes, boats, airplanes, farm equipment, and construction equipment.

54. HABITAT FOR HUMANITY CARS FOR HOMES:
https://www.habitat.org/support/how-to-donate-your-car
What they do: build and rehabilitate houses for families in need.

What they need: cars, trucks, boats, RVs, motorcycles, and construction equipment.

55. NATIONAL KIDNEY FOUNDATION KIDNEY CARS:
https://www.kidney.org/support/kidneycars
What they do: Fund public health and professional education, vital patient and community services, organ donation programs, and medical research to prevent kidney disease.

What they need: Cars, vans, trucks, and boats.

56. PURPLE HEART:
https://cardonation.purpleheartcars.org/
What they do: provide a variety of programs for wounded and disabled veterans and their families.

What they need: cars, trucks, RVs and boats.

MISCELLANEOUS:

57. NATIONAL FURNITURE BANK:

http://furniturebanks.org/

What they do: Provide beds, tables, chairs, and other crucial home furnishing to over 100,000 people in need each year.

What they need: Beds, dressers, nightstands, tables, chairs, sofas, lamps, and more.

58. ST. JUDE'S RANCH:

https://stjudesranch.org/recycled-card-program/

What they do: Serve all abused, abandoned, and neglected children and families in a safe, homelike environment.

What they need: Used greeting cards.

CHAPTER NINE
Upgrade Your Lifestyle

"The secret to happiness is not found in seeking more,
but in developing the capacity to enjoy less."

SOCRATES

What comes to mind when you hear the word upgrade? First-class airline seats or upgraded travel perks? These are wonderful perks and surprises that we love to receive. They are often unexpected and considerably enhance our experiences. By definition, upgrade means to improve the quality of something or to raise something to a higher standard. It goes without saying that we are extremely grateful when these opportunities come our way to experience life at a higher level.

Ten years ago, my dear friends invited me to their son's wedding weekend in Beverly Hills. Excited to share in this special celebration, I decided to splurge on a room at a five-star hotel in the heart of Beverly Hills. Upon checking in at the front desk, the general manager overheard me say how excited I was to be staying there and that I had decided to treat myself to a special weekend. He immediately smiled and welcomed me. He then asked me a question that I had never been asked before at a hotel. "Madame, what are your favorite colors? I want to select the perfect room for you." I quickly told him coral, soft yellow, and sage green. He then told the desk clerk who had been helping me that he would like to personally handle my reservation. Within minutes, he said, "Come with me, I want to be sure that you are pleased with the accommodation I have selected for you." As he escorted me to my room, I was both pleased and surprised by this special attention.

As he opened the door, I was delighted to walk through my stunning three-room suite with private balcony overlooking Rodeo Drive. It was as if this suite had been designed just for me! Coral sofas, soft yellow walls, designer pillows, and area rugs with coral yellow and sage were scattered throughout—and there were fresh yellow and coral roses in every room. Needless to say, I was thrilled with my "over the top" upgrade and with the exceptional personal service from the general manager himself. That turned out to be the first of several other unexpected treats I received throughout the weekend.

The gifts that keep on giving

While this most memorable "upgrade experience" left a lasting impression on me even after these many years, the actual upgrades were temporary and fleeting. One and done. The types of lifestyle upgrades that I write and speak about are permanent, ongoing, generative, and life-altering. They are gifts that keep on giving. When implemented, the lifestyle upgrades I share will not only enhance the quality of your lifestyle but they will also raise the bar for how you actually experience yourself and your life for the rest of your life.

Imagine living an upgraded lifestyle every day of your life where you choose based on your values and what matters most to you. You won't have to depend on others to surprise you with intermittent lifestyle upgrades. Your lifestyle upgrades are completely within your control every day and it all begins with the choices you make simply by changing your thinking, expectations, attitude, behavior, and performance. John Maxwell's Six Simple Steps to Change Your Life changed my life and they can change yours too. It begins with changing the way you think.

Six Steps to Change Your Life—John Maxwell

1. When you change your *thinking*, you will change your *beliefs*.
2. When you change your *beliefs*, you will change your *expectations*.
3. When you change your *expectations*, you will change your *attitude*.
4. When you change your *attitude*, you will change your *behavior*.
5. When you change your behavior, you will change your performance.
6. When you change your performance, you will change your life.

A seed was planted

My experience in Senegal—of people having very little but being happy—planted a seed; a seed that grew into a longing for a simpler, more fulfilling life with less.

1. My thinking had been that I needed more stuff to be happy. I had fallen into the consumer trap that more is better than less. I was in a death spiral. Howard C. Samuels, Psy. D. licensed therapist, calls it the disease of more.

I changed my belief about needing more.

Owning less allows me to live more with fewer possessions. I have fewer distractions, allowing me to focus on people and things that bring me true happiness and fulfillment. I changed my belief about needing more. Owning less allows me to live more

2. When I changed my beliefs, I changed my expectations
I stopped buying more and started giving my stuff away to people who needed or wanted it. I not only believed I could live with less, I now knew I could and wanted to live with less.

3. When I changed my expectations, my attitude changed.
Nothing was going to stop me from having that simpler life with less. I became unstoppable.

4. When I changed my attitude, I gained momentum, built a team, and was in action every day to have what I wanted most.
I now knew I could live more with less.

5. When I changed my behavior, I realized I was accomplishing something I previously thought impossible... giving away 95% of my stuff and moving from 5,000 square feet to 867 square feet.
I stepped out of my comfort zone and upped my game and performance so I could have that simple joy-filled life with less.

6. When I chose to change my performance, I played big instead of small.
My life was changed forever. I upgraded my life and lifestyle by choosing to live with less. I'm now living in a tiny jewel-box apartment with 5% of what I once owned. I went from a life full of possessions to a life filled with meaning. I have all I want and all I need and I've never been happier. I'm living abundantly with less.

- What is your dream?
- How can you upgrade your lifestyle to live more each day?
- What do you need more of?
- What do you need less of?

Downsizing is easier than you might expect. Once you begin the process and gain momentum, you, too, will question why you bought so much in the first place. Living with less has an unexpected outcome. It provides room for a more meaningful and fulfilling life.

I have compiled a comprehensive list of LIFESTYLE UPGRADES that you can choose to implement immediately or integrate gradually. These upgrades, when implemented, will have a lasting impact on your happiness and quality of life.

31 LIFESTYLE UPGRADES THAT WILL CHANGE YOUR LIFE

1. Enjoy life on the skinny branches

"In the end, we only regret the chances we did not take, the relationships we were afraid to have, and decisions we waited too long to make."—Lewis Carroll

Living life outside of your comfort zone is one of the most exciting places on earth to live life to the fullest. When you challenge your own beliefs, behaviors, and habits and climb out onto life's skinny branches, you see your world through a completely new lens. It allows you to see and experience life fully.

"If you get the chance, take it. If it changes your life, let it. No one said it would be easy. They just promised it would be worth it."—Dr. Seuss

Our days are numbered. Why wait? Show up afraid. Be courageous. Dare yourself to seek new experiences that will challenge you and help you grow beyond your wildest dreams. I am challenging myself to take improvisation classes. I am scared and excited at the same time... a good scared.

What will you challenge yourself to do today that scares you so that a year from now you will be unrecognizable?

2. Unleash your inner child

Moving to the city awakened a part of me that laid dormant for a long, long time... it unleashed the inner child in me.

On an early morning walk with a friend, I discovered a playground I had not seen before. I immediately approached the set of swings that were calling my name. A few minutes later, a young boy joined me for what quickly became a swinging competition. As he swung higher, so did I. I felt an inner child-like joy that I hadn't felt in years.

Suddenly, the young boy stopped swinging, looked directly into my eyes and asked, "Why are you here?!" As the mother of boys myself, I smiled at his seemingly harsh comment and replied right back to him, "Because I want to be a kid like you!" His mother stood at a distance laughing hysterically at our interaction. Fortunately, my friend captured that early morning swing experience in the photo below. In that moment, I rediscovered something that had been missing in my life—pure child-like joy and spontaneity.

For me, living in the city is like living on a

SHE DESIGNED A LIFE THAT SHE LOVED

AND SO CAN YOU!

playground. Opportunities abound to discover, to be curious, explore, learn, play, and practice... lessons learned in childhood and fortunately, not totally forgotten.

What a gift it is to rediscover the feeling of being unleashed, of being true to the inner child inside! Why not awaken the inner child in you? It takes years off your life.

3. Savor, anticipate, and create special moments.

It is often said, "It's the little things that matter most." Learn to be fully present and engaged in life's everyday moments. Capture vivid mental images and strong emotional connections to those special moments so you can recall and relive them in the future.

Many years ago, our dad had a massive stroke that left him partially paralyzed, restricted to a wheelchair, and unable to speak. In spite of his handicaps, he had love in his heart, a constant smile on his face, and one "good arm" that he wrapped around my shoulder for some of the most memorable conversations I have ever experienced. I talked. He listened with his eyes and responded with a smile, a tear, or a squeeze on my shoulder. These cherished moments make me smile every time I think of those father-daughter talks. He is no longer with us, but the memories of those special moments are seared in my heart forever, contributing to the richness of my life and overall wellbeing.

When was the last time you slowed down to fully experience the beauty of a sunrise or sunset, the laughter of someone close to you, or even the tickle of a puppy's cold nose on your face? These moments are priceless and surpass any monetary value. Slow down. Be in the moment. Create memories that will last your lifetime.

4. Laugh out loud everyday

Laughter is a universal language that connects people and strips away the outside veneer. It is irresistible and contagious. It feels good to laugh out loud. It improves mental and physical health and wellbeing. It significantly reduces stress. The old adage, "laughter is the best medicine," while not scientifically proven, seems to ring true on many counts: laughter will add years to your life and life to your years.

When my sons began courting their future spouses, my motherly instincts confirmed they were "the ones" for my sons when I witnessed how they regularly made each other laugh out loud. The language of laughter and the language of love is a surefire way to live life to the fullest each day.

5. Be a lifelong learner

"Live as if you were to die tomorrow. Learn as if you were to live forever." –Mahatma Gandhi

Learning is a journey that never ends. Every day is a new opportunity to learn, grow, live an extraordinary life and develop your passions. Challenge yourself to disrupt the status quo and think differently so you can reach new heights and achieve new goals. Experience progress, breakthroughs, and create new opportunities to improve yourself and the world. Embrace change, experience failure, and learn from all of it. Surround yourself with others who know more than you in areas you want to grow. Never rest, never settle.

6. Adopt the mindset of enough

There is a rich abundance, quiet contentment, and profound peace of mind when you embrace "I have all I want and all I need. I am enough." Happiness lies within you, not in comparing yourself to others, what you have or don't have. The comparison game limits your ability to be free to discover and live your life according to what you value. It will allow you to live to your fullest potential, not someone else's. Experience the peace and joy in having enough and being enough.

7. Be you. The one and only authentic you.
Why try to be anyone or anything else? It's much easier to be just you—all that you are, all that you are not. Own your unique greatness, your voice, and your leadership.

The world awaits. It takes courage to be vulnerable, imperfect, and irresistibly you. Just do it.

Stepping out onto the TEDx stage in November 2017 was the moment I finally allowed myself to stand in my own leadership, use my voice to tell my story and make a much bigger difference than I had ever imagined before. Accepting God's challenge to be the voice for the impact of living with less has made me more vibrantly alive and self-expressed than ever before.

Own all of who you are and who you are meant to be. Share you with the world. It is like no other adventure you have ever taken.

8. Embrace the attitude of gratitude
It is a funny thing about life. Once you start noticing how much you already have and once you embrace being grateful for it, you begin to lose sight of the things you lack. Make a list of who and what you are grateful for and why. Keep it in a special place where you will be reminded. Add to it daily. Write a thank you note or tell them in person. They will be changed by your kindness, acknowledgement and gratitude, and so will you.

9. Start investing in MORE meaningful experiences. Stop wasting money on MORE meaningless stuff.

"The best things in life are not things at all."– Art Buchwald

+ Contrast the temporary thrill of buying a new expensive car with the permanent impact of spending quality time with your family at the kitchen table each night.

+ Contrast the momentary pleasure of receiving yet another expensive gift that you will rarely use from your spouse with the lasting gift of quality time together and intimate conversations at a surprise romantic getaway weekend.

+ There is no comparison for which one of those choices brings the deeper, longer-lasting memories.

+ Meaningful experiences are priceless and memorable because they elicit deep human connection that make us feel happy, valued, and loved.

+ The paradox of accumulating more "stuff" is that it eventually leaves us feeling empty and unfulfilled. We can have all the money in the world yet feel poor. We can have an extraordinary amount of beautiful things and still experience a hunger and yearning for more. It is a never-ending cycle.

+ "Having it all" starts with seeking experiences that are meaningful, fulfilling, and priceless.

10. Don't let failure stop you. Let it increase your desire to succeed.

"You never fail until you stop trying." Albert Einstein

Some of our biggest breakthroughs come from failures. Think of failures you may have had in your lifetime. What did you learn from them?

When we take responsibility for our failure, when we accept and own what didn't work, and when we take the opportunity to learn from it, a breakthrough is likely just around the corner.

As an entrepreneur, I have had many opportunities to fail. It has made me extremely resilient and fearless. Failure is, in some ways, fun. Yes, fun. I accept the unexpected challenges and twists and turns that come with living on the edge of always trying new things. Some ideas work and some do not. I have learned to reframe the word failure and simply look at it differently as a new opportunity to be curious and learn. The fun begins when you continue to challenge yourself to keep trying.

11. Try something new each day

- When was the last time you did something for the first time?
- What scares you that you have always wished you were courageous enough to try?
- What is on your bucket list that is outside of your comfort zone?

If your life is on autopilot, if your daily routine bores you to tears, if you crave variety and a more adventurous life, then try something new each day.

When I lived in the beautiful rolling hills of Chester County, Pennsylvania, there were at least 10 ways I could drive to my office. Each one was even more beautiful than the next. As I got into my car in the morning to drive to my office, I often chose a new route just to keep life interesting. Now that I live in Philadelphia, I still find myself trying something new each day.

When I first moved to the city, I said yes to just about every invitation I received: theater, restaurants, churches, museums, and meet-ups. Of course, saying yes to everything nearly wore me out, so in my second year, I was much more discriminating about what I agreed to do, but I still found myself doing something new each day, large or small.

Stepping out of my comfort zone has become fun and part of who I am. Constant exploration definitely has its benefits.

5 Benefits of trying something new each day:

1. It increases your creativity and becomes an inspiration for even more ideas.
2. It provides daily opportunities to learn something new and meet new people.
3. It invites an open mind and new perspective.
4. It helps you develop an appreciation and excitement for stepping out of your comfort zone.
5. It improves your mind, mood, and zest for life.

Trying something new each day changes you. It challenges you to be creative, think differently, and embrace life to the fullest. So when I finally stepped onto that improv stage, it reminded me that I chose to dare myself to do that!

12. Live experientially. It's the journey, not the destination.

As a lifestyle design expert, I encourage people to immerse themselves and engage fully to experience living life to the fullest each day. Experiences help us connect with others, with our environment, and with ourselves in a meaningful way. It is a hands-on way of learning about life. Participate more fully in your own life each day to get on the court rather than sitting on the sidelines. Stop being an observer of your own life. It is where you get to see, touch, feel, and experience each day and moment. Experience firsthand what an adventure your life really is.

13. Live expectantly.

Give yourself permission to expect that great things will happen in your life. Expect that miracles will happen. Expect God to provide all you want and all you need.

This is a new mindset and behavior for me. I was afraid to dream too big because I feared failure or that it wouldn't happen at all. Since I have been practicing the art of living expectantly, abundance is showing up in every area of my life. I realize now that it is my choice to expect, to believe that great things will continue to happen in my life. It is about dreaming big and then dreaming even bigger. It's about thinking of all the things that can go right instead of all the things that can go wrong. It's about having faith, trusting that God will provide everything I need to accomplish my dreams. It is about being all in, committing to live the life I love and then sharing that dream with others so they can have the life they love too if they choose to.

Develop a habit of asking for what you want and then expecting it to happen.

14. Lifestyle prototyping.

Have you ever wondered what it would be like to…

> Live in Italy or France or Africa for a year.
>
> Live in Paris for a month so you feel like a Parisian.
>
> Live on a ship and teach baby boomers how to write their legacy book.
>
> Live in a major city where you can walk everywhere.

What stops you from having these dreams?

Are you tempted to put your toe in the water of one of your dreams to test it before you buy?

Are they really such crazy ideas or are they logical strategies for finding the perfect fit for having diverse experiences that are exciting, fun, and challenging?

Several months ago, I told my sons on July 1, 2019 that I will become a digital nomad, traveling around the world. My first three months will be in the south of France, Italy, and Spain. Then I will spend my second three months doing service work in West Africa. The next six months are not yet planned, but tentatively India, Israel, and Nepal. I was so proud of my boys for not thinking I was crazy. They know that I love adventure, travel, culture, people, and new experiences. They know I am willing to step out of my comfort zone for the sake of the life-changing learning experiences that I will have.

As a lifestyle designer, I am prototyping or testing a new lifestyle. It is putting my toe in the water to explore, learn, experience, and enhance the quality of my own life. As the designer of your own life, what do you want to prototype?

15. Connect, build, and nurture relationships.

We are wired for human connection. Without it, life is empty and meaningless. Fostering connections and nurturing relationships is the key to real happiness and a successful life. Human beings need to belong, and to feel loved and engaged in life. Taking time to connect with and spend time with those who matter most to us is the essence of a life well lived.

According to Harvard's Grant and Glueck's Study, which tracked 700 participants for over 75 years, they concluded that the key to long-term happiness and fulfillment comes down to the quality of our relationships. Invest your time in relationships, share your hopes, dreams, and fears. They are priceless.

16. Balancing life and work.

"Never get so busy making a living that you forget to make a life."
–Dolly Parton

Where do you draw the line when we live in a culture where we can work 24/7? Is it technology's fault that we are so connected, or are we responsible for checking our devices and laptops at the door so we can spend quality time with our families? When we fail to disconnect from work and our devices, we become disconnected from what matters most. Setting boundaries between work and life allows us to better manage our time and energy, preventing the proverbial stress and burnout. If you don't have enough time for what matters, just stop doing things that don't.

Prioritize what matters most. Create structures and schedules that work. Leverage technology to manage your time and energy. Have time for work, family, social events, and personal interests. You will never feel truly satisfied by work until you're satisfied with your life.

17. Make time for you.

Self-care
Take care of yourself first or you won't be any good for others. Learn to say yes to what you need for your own health, happiness, and wellbeing. Know what you need to relieve stress, recalibrate, and restore balance in your life. Listen to your body, whether it's quiet time alone, praying, journaling, taking a hot bath, or going for a run.

Self-care is an action that your future self will thank you for. Invest in yourself.

Self-aware
"Being extremely honest with yourself is a good exercise."
–Sigmund Freud

A high level of self-awareness is a strong indicator of overall success in life. Self-awareness is about being willing to explore areas of your life that you are feeling nagging discontent about the way things are or areas that you are longing for things to be different or better. By focusing attention on yourself, becoming aware of your thoughts and feelings, including negative emotions, you can evaluate where you can take action to improve those areas in your life.

18. Live intentionally.
Life is a series of tiny miracles each day, but do we even notice them?

Living intentionally is about taking small daily actions that are thoughtfully aligned with your vision, values, and beliefs. Stand in your commitments, your why. The choices you make moment by moment will help you live the life you love. Live your life on purpose. Notice the tiny miracles each day.

Life is really quite simple. Be intentional about what you do and who you are spending time with. Hold on to what matters most to you, let go of what doesn't.

19. Fail better
"Failure is only the opportunity to more intelligently begin again."
–Henry Ford

Change how you think about failure and you will become fearless and unstoppable. Failure is simply an opportunity to learn from our mistakes. Failure is one of our greatest sources of learning.

20. Stay in your lane.
Play to your strengths. Why waste time fixing your weaknesses when you could focus on building your strengths. Once you discover your unique brilliance, nurture it and spend time in that lane. Take advantage of opportunities that leverage your brilliance. Know what you do well, what gives you life, what lights you up. Focus on those things that motivate you to perform at your highest level—that will lead you to a happier, more fulfilling life.

21. Live a debt-free life
Living debt-free provides you the freedom and power to create a life that you really want. It's an opportunity to take control of your life, to make decisions based on confidence in your future and ability to have the life you want for yourself and your family. Debt-free living is a life-changing lifestyle.

22. Downsize and declutter.
Live a rich and abundant life with less. Downsize and declutter your life by removing all unnecessary possessions and things that distract you from what you value most. You will have more time, money, and freedom to make room for what matters more. Make room for things that matter by removing everything that doesn't. You will never be the same again.

23. Be. Here. Now.
"We are always getting ready to live but never really living."
–Ralph Waldo Emerson

Stop mourning the past. Stop worrying about the future. Choosing to live in the past or the future robs you of the enjoyment of today. Commit to staying centered and focused on the present. It connects you to yourself and to those around you. Embracing life's "now moments" is a priceless gift you can give yourself and others.

24. Take consistent action daily toward the life you want
Take consistent daily action toward the life you want. Success is found in daily routines, habits, and actions even in the face of resistance and setback. Daily actions and daily results are cumulative. They build momentum. They help us never give up and stay in the game.

25. Make your time count. Live your dash.
"A man who dares to waste one hour time has not discovered the value of life."–Charles Darwin

We all have the same amount of minutes and hours in a day. Like money, our time is ours to invest or to waste.

Are you investing your valuable time by making each priceless moment count?

Are you wasting too much of your time reacting to things that don't add value to your life? If you don't have time to do what matters, stop doing the things that don't.

Every choice you make impacts the quality of your life and happiness.

Once you begin to think of time as a precious gift, you will never be the same again.

26. Practice journaling

The practice of regularly recording your thoughts, dreams, goals, memories, and experiences helps track evolution of your life journey. It helps you track where you were, where you are, and inspires where you might be going. By reflecting on your life, by journaling the challenges you are facing, you can monitor progress, keep yourself on track, and even notice little miracles that occur each day. It will help you create the vision for the life you really want, the one that you get to create by living intentionally each day.

Daily journaling helps you discover areas of discontent about the way things are, as well as the longing for the way you want things to be in your life. It's an opportunity to mind map significant ideas and inspirations that you might have, to create small or major goals for your life. It's also an opportunity to reflect on, to celebrate and to be grateful for just how awesome your life already is.

27. Embrace the habit of reading

"Reading is to the mind what exercise is to the body."
–Joseph Addison

Reading adds value to our lives, which lasts a lifetime. It is a gift that keeps on giving. It expands our horizons, it exercises our brain, and it opens our mind. Reading helps us to develop a broader view and deeper perspective. It helps us to form big ideas and new concepts, and helps us connect the dots. To develop a habit of reading requires diligence, patience, and determination.

When you don't think you have time to read, consider making an investment in yourself by making reading a priority.

28. Create your vision board

"The sky isn't the limit. Your belief system is."
—A Buddhist quote

The Law of Attraction:
If you focus on what you want, you will attract what you want. A vision board is a simple visual tool that will help you visualize and serve as a reminder of what it is that you want to attract in your life. By having a clear visual reminder, it helps you to stay focused on that vision so that it will become your reality. Activate your dreams.

Create a vision board for the life you love.

29. Ask What If

Be curious. Wonder. Dream. Ask "what if questions," then ask it again. Continue to expand your thinking and your world. Share your dreams with others. Pretend there are no limits or conditions that would hold you back. Play the scenarios out in your mind and then try them out.

30. Choose joy!

Don't wait for things to get easier, simpler, or better. Life will always have its complications and circumstances that try to stop you. By choosing and experiencing that child-like joy each day, life may not be easier or simpler, but choosing joy, no matter what, just makes life better.

UPGRADING YOUR LIFESTYLE ONE LAST WORD

31. Never Quit

I have been fearless for a very long time. As a young teenager, I had a clipping of this poem, "Don't Quit," taped to the inside of my closet door, which meant I read it several times daily.

While I hadn't yet experienced too many failures at that young age, other than the poor science grade on my report card, it was fortuitous that I had those words etched in my brain. Those words prepared me well for future failures that I would experience as an adult.

Ingrained in my brain, "success is failure turned inside out," helped me develop my own set of rules to live by when facing failure—or when faced with the desire to give up.

Those words helped me not only combat failure but also develop a hard and fast mantra, "**EXPECT TO SUCCEED**".

Don't Quit by John Greenleaf Whittier

When things go wrong as they sometimes will,
When the road you're trudging seems all up hill,
When the funds are low and the debts are high
And you want to smile, but you have to sigh,
When care is pressing you down a bit,
Rest if you must, but don't you quit.
Life is strange with its twists and turns
As every one of us sometimes learns
And many a failure comes about
When he might have won had he stuck it out;
Don't give up though the pace seems slow—
You may succeed with another blow.
Success is failure turned inside out—

The silver tint of the clouds of doubt,
And you never can tell just how close you are,
It may be near when it seems so far;
So stick to the fight when you're hardest hit—
It's when things seem worst that you must not quit.

Regardless of how difficult my circumstances were at various times in my life, I always expected myself to figure it out and find a way to succeed. Through it all, I kept believing in myself and God, trusting that He would provide all I needed to achieve my goals.

Fearlessness became second nature. So did resilience. If it didn't work the first time, I would try again and again.

You don't need to be upgraded to first class to upgrade your lifestyle (although those fun little perks are great). Opportunities to experience your life each day at a whole new level are all around you… you just have to open your eyes.

You don't need to change the world around you; you just need to change the way you see your world.

Life's simple pleasures, life's little miracles are all around you. All you have to do is notice them. To see them through your new life lens and then appreciate that the power to change your world exists within you—the choices you make each day to experience yourself and your life at a whole new level.

It's really that simple.

You can upgrade your lifestyle at any time and it doesn't have to cost you a dime! It's a gift that keeps on giving.

31-Day Challenge to Upgrade Your Lifestyle

OPTION A
Select one lifestyle upgrade each day for 31 days. Practice experiencing yourself and your life at a whole new level.

OPTION B
Pick one of the 31 Lifestyle Upgrades. Practice experiencing that upgrade each day for 31 days.

I would love to hear from you and how this practice changed your life.

CHAPTER TEN

Fully Live Your 3^Rd Act

If someone told me a year ago that I would be spending the month of July in the South of France, **Working 3 days and Play 4 days**, I would not have believed them. It was not on my radar, nor was it within the realm of possibility for me. If anything, it was a very distant dream on my bucket list that might happen... someday.

But then, something crazy happened last November. While writing this book, "Downsize Your Life Upgrade Your Lifestyle," I have been learning and growing too... listening for what I wanted next in my own life. I knew that I wanted more, like many other baby boomers, but I wasn't sure what that was.

I had already downsized my physical space and I was experiencing the tremendous life-giving freedom as a result of living with so much less. I had let go of so many of the things that had previously held me back from doing what really mattered most to me. I was now free to discover new things, to pursue my dreams and passions. I had also entered the 3rd act of my life and I wanted to make the most of this season of my life. I definitely wanted to use my talents and skills to continue to impact many through interior design and lifestyle design.

There was a new sense of urgency to the way I wanted to live my life. And like many other baby boomers, I love what I do and I refuse to retire into the so-called sunset years. I want to create something new, vibrant, and exciting that will make a difference for many while I still can. Most of all, I wanted to live life to the fullest and share what I learned with others so they, too, can design and live the life they love.

Even though I had done much of the work to downsize my life so I could live a simpler, less cluttered, and more meaningful life, last November, I suddenly realized that I had not given myself permission to dream big and fully live the life I most wanted.

This was a game-changing moment for me. I began to wonder, *what if...*

- What if... I took that long journey to the South of France that I had always dreamed of and still managed to work 3 and play 4?

- What if... I could make my dream a reality. Not someday, but one day soon in the not-too-distant future?

- What if... I made my other dreams, both big and small, come to life... the ones I relegated to my someday list?

My mantra became... "If not now, when?"

That was on November 22, 2018. I remember that day so clearly because it opened my eyes to a whole new way of living that I wanted not just for myself but to share with others. Those magic words, *"what if,"* changed my whole mindset to *"why not now?"*

After all, we all have an expiration date and someday may never come. What if I could design the life I love living each day? I began to dream of all the things I could do now that I was no longer burdened with excess in my life and now that I had given myself the permission and freedom to act on my dreams. Nothing was going to hold me back any longer from persuing what mattered most to me. I had completely redefined what success meant to me... and it definitely wasn't about accumulating more. True success had come to mean having more love, more inner peace, and more contentment.

It was about finding happiness in the little things each day, having a higher quality of relationships, and being authentically me. Saying no, setting limits and boundaries, guarding each precious moment as if it were my last had all become second nature to me. Saying yes to only the things that matter most to me and saying no to everything else that doesn't.

The seed for the idea to Work 3 days and Play 4 in the South of France had been planted. It continued to grow in my mind, in my imagination, and in my heart. I didn't know how to make it happen, but I knew it would. Work 3, Play 4 had been a business model we had been testing in-house for several years, but we had never tried to implement it remotely. What once seemed impossible because of fear and limiting beliefs began to disappear. Other objections began to disappear. As my dream became clearer, my vision for working remotely while traveling for fun in the South of France for thirty days gained momentum. As I began to share my idea with family, friends, and colleagues, my vision was quickly becoming my reality. What I once thought impossible was not becoming probable and would soon become inevitable.

In early January 2019, I shared my idea with my team, and rather than telling me it was a crazy idea, they embraced it. We started to brainstorm how we could make it work. From January through the end of June, we refined and reworked the Work 3, Play 4 business model, putting systems and structures in place that would allow my business to fully function and grow while I was prototyping the Work 3, Play 4 lifestyle business model abroad.

On July 1, 2019, I arrived in Marseilles, France, just eight months after I decided to design and live the life I was meant to live. As I write this final chapter of my book, I will also be finishing my life-changing journey here in France. I upgraded my life by acting on my dream even though it scared me and even though I once thought it was impossible. Having the courage to push through those fears has helped me to see myself and my life differently. This new lens has inspired and emboldened me to continue following my own dreams while inspiring and encouraging others to follow their own dreams, having the courage to say "yes" to the life they were meant to live.

The secret to living life fully each day for the rest of your life is to realize that the best days of your life have not even happened yet!

Acknowledgments

This book, *Downsize Your Life, Upgrade Your Lifestyle*, holds a special place in my heart. It represents many years of personal and professional growth, training, life lessons, experiences... and multiple reinventions!

I have many to thank who have been on this journey with me and who have contributed in significant ways. For those of you who know my story, you know that my life has not always been easy. And yes, with your love, wisdom and support I grew stronger from those life experiences. My downsizing journey and this book represent new life and another fresh start.

Thanks to each of you this book is possible. Designing and living my new life... by design.

I would like to personally acknowledge and thank the following people and groups of people who inspired me, encouraged me, and stayed with me through it all!

Pauline Tartaglia, wise beyond your years, you are an unstoppable force of nature who knows no boundaries. Thank you for traveling with me on this journey for the past 10 years. You have been an integral part of our team and of your growth as a designer, business woman, trusted advisor, loyal friend and even as my surrogate daughter.

Thank you for always being willing to explore new ideas, for being a sounding board, and for pushing back. Thank you for always "figuring it out" even though you may have not known how to do something new. Thank you for always keeping us focused on our big picture goals and for making them happen.

Most of all, thank you for your love, friendship, and unwavering support.

Nancy Ippoliti, as one of our newest design team members, you provide a valuable balance of experience, creativity, and wisdom. Thank you for your fresh ideas, insight and voice. Thank you for joining us on this journey as we continue to expand for "what's next" in service to our clients.

A special thanks for my mentors, coaches, advisors, teams and communities.

My Downsizing Team, where this journey began. You made the seemingly impossible task of downsizing possible and fun. Thank you Sean, Kevin, Nat, Barb, Mary, Karen, M2, Rob and the Eagle Scouts and many others who participated.

Gerry Lantz, of the National Speakers Academy, thank you for opening my eyes to the world and business of speaking, for your coaching, and for being my cheerleader. Also a special thanks to my NSA 1.0 and 2.0 team members for your inspiration and support.

Dr. Jim Smith, Jr., CSP, National Speakers Association, to one of the greatest speakers I know. I want to be like you someday. Thank you for sharing your talent and wisdom.

Steve Harrison, Bill Harrison, Geoffrey Berwind, and Martha Bullen, of Quantum Leap, thanks to all of your for making my head spin. The Quantum Leap programs and coaching provided the roadmap I needed for a successful book launch and marketing. Your events, coaching, and templates have been a valuable source of expertise from proven experts. I am grateful to be a part of the QL family. Many have become lifelong friends.

Judy Cohen, Quantum Leap Mastermind Coach and to our fellow members, thank you for being a resource for our progress and growth and for standing for each of us to succeed in our perspective businesses.

Ajit George, TEDx Wilmington and your professional team of organizers, thank you for the opportunity to share my big idea worth spreading on the TEDx stage. Thank you for your inspirational leadership, and for your kind, compassionate, no-nonsense coaching.

Lisa Arko, Landmark Worldwide, thank you for being such a tenacious coach, for helping me discover my voice, my power, and my leadership. You are a forever friend. A special thanks to my team members who lifted each other up when needed.

To all of my fellow board members and friends at Fresh Start Scholarship Foundation and Great Dames, Inc. it is an honor and privilege to serve with women who are passionate about making a difference for women and girls. Together, we pave the way for their better futures.

And for many others who inspired me and influenced me with your books, blogs, events, speaking, podcasts and online courses, you may not know me, but I know you and I want each of you to know that I acknowledge you for what you do to transform lives. Thank you for your passion to change lives. You changed mine. Thank you.

A special thanks to Joshua Becker: *The More of Less*, Rick Warren: *Purpose Driven*, Brene Brown: *The Gifts of Imperfection*, Mary Morrissey: *Dream Builder Live*, John Maxwell: *Power of*

Significance, Linda Ellis: *Live Your Dash*, Luann Cahn: *I Dare Me*, Rachel Hollis: *Girl Wash Your Face*, Need James: *Attention Pays*.

And most of all, thank God for my gifts and for being with me on this journey. You make all things possible.

Resources That Inspired Me

The More of Less: Finding the Life You Want Under Everything You Own—Joshua Becker

Soulful Simplicity: How Living with Less Can Lead to So Much More—Courtney Carver

Disrupt Aging: A Bold New Path to Living Your Best Life at Every Age—Jo Ann Jenkins, CEO AARP

The Gifts of Imperfection: Let Go of Who You Think You're Supposed to Be and Embrace Who You Are—Brene Brown

Your Best Year Ever: A 5-Step Plan for Achieving Your Most Important Goals—Michael Hyatt

I Dare Me: How I Rebooted and Recharged My Life by Doing Something New Every Day—Lu Ann Cahn

Eat, Pray, Love: One Woman's Search for Everything Across Italy, India and Indonesia—Elizabeth Gilbert

Live Your Dash: Make Every Moment Matter—Linda Ellis

Power of Significance: How Purpose Changes Your Life—John C. Maxwell

Power of Less: The Fine Art of Limiting Yourself to the Essential... in Business and in Life—Leo Babauta

Girl, Wash Your Face: Stop Believing the Lies About Who You Are So You Can Become Who You Were Meant to Be—Rachel Hollis and Thomas Nelson

The Happiness Project—Gretchen Rubin

Purposeful Retirement: How to Bring Happiness and Meaning to Your Retirement—Hyrum W. Smith

Book Club Questions

If you have a book club, and you would like ideas for group discussion, feel free to reference the following book club questions to start your discussion:

Please make sure **you register below** to win a virtual book club discussion with Rita.

Reference these questions to start your book club group discussion:

1. Does this book speak to a challenge you face or expect to face in the next few years?

2. If so, what obstacles and barriers are you experiencing? What has helped you to move forward?

3. What did you find most helpful about this book?

4. What feelings did the book evoke for you?

5. What was a favorite idea or quote from the book? Why?

6. What inspirations would you like to share that have allowed you to upgrade your life?

7. What other books have you read on this topic that you can recommend to others?

8. How will you apply something you've learned from this book to your life?

9. How could downsizing impact the quality of your life?

10. **If you had the chance to ask the author one question, what would that be?**

Register to Win

Have Rita attend your book club for 1 hour virtuallyto answer questions and share additional insights.

Drawings will take place once per month.

Go here to register: www.ritawilkins.com/bookclub

Tell Us About Your Downsizing Journey

I really want to know. Others really want and need to know. We can all learn from each other.

You might have already completed your downsizing journey, while others might just be starting theirs.

- Your story could be what someone else needs to hear right now.
- Your story could inspire someone to begin their own downsizing journey.
- Your story could be the one that encourages someone to keep on going.

Make a difference for others today by sharing your story on our website, www.RitaWilkins.com/TellUsAboutYourDownsizingJourney. Use your story and your voice to inspire, encourage, and empower someone else to live with less so they can live with more.

Use these questions to help craft your own powerful personal story of downsizing, the experience, and the impact downsizing and living with less has made on your life.

1. What was your most difficult challenge? Why?

2. What other challenges did you face along the way?

3. How did you overcome them?

4. Why did you downsize (i.e. empty nest, divorce)?

5. What did you do with all of your "stuff" (i.e., sell, donate, trash, keep, other)?

6. How did you deal with the emotions of letting go of things that once mattered to you?

7. Did you have a team assist you (family, friends, other)?

8. What are 3 tips, tools or strategies that worked for you? Explain.

9. How has downsizing and living with less impacted the quality of your life?

10. What did you learn about yourself during this journey?

11. Anything else you would like to add?

12. What would you say to a friend who is thinking about downsizing?

Your story matters. Thank you for contributing to the lives of others.

Register to Win a 30 Minute Call with Rita

Ask her questions. Get coaching.
Tell her more about your downsizing journey.

Drawings will take place once per month.

Go here to register: www.RitaWilkins.com/ TellUsAboutYourDownsizingJourney

About the Author

Rita Wilkins, also known as "The Downsizing Designer," is a nationally recognized interior design and lifestyle design expert, and TEDx speaker. In addition to having designed thousands of residential and commercial interiors all over the United States, she spent the last three decades studying, observing, and impacting how people live, work and play in their environments.

She is a master of reinventing lives, including her own. Several years ago she was profoundly impacted by a trip to a third world country, "where people had so little but they were happy." A few years later, Rita downsized from her 5,000 square foot home to a 867 square foot jewel box apartment in Philadelphia. She gave away 95% of her possessions to people who needed them or wanted them. She is now living with 5% of what she once owned—and has never been happier.

Rita is the real deal. She walked the walk and when she downsized she, too, experienced the pain of letting go of possessions that she had emotional attachment to. But she also experienced the life-changing benefits and joy of living a simpler life with less. She now has more time, money and freedom to pursue what matters most.

In her book, Rita uses the same design principles she has successfully used for over 35 years to help readers think differently about their own lives. She has the rare ability to help people, "see through their invisible walls" of fear, and discover what prevents them from having the life they really want—and deserve. She is an expert in helping people reimagine, reinvent and redesign their lives!

Rita is a popular guest on radio, TV, and podcasts reaching hundreds of thousands of listeners, viewers, and readers across the US. A highly sought after thought leader on the baby boomer generation and the movement to live abundantly with less, she is a regular contributor to business and lifestyle publications and blogs.

A dynamic transformational speaker, she authentically connects with her audiences, inspiring them and empowering them to live the life they love… by design.

Rita lives in the heart of historic Philadelphia, loves her new life as a city girl. She is the proud mother of two happily married sons and is excited about being a new grandmother. Always creating something new and challenging, she just spent 30 days in the south of France prototyping a new location independent lifestyle, Work 3 and Play 4.

If you want to learn more visit: www.RitaWilkins.com or contact Rita directly at RitaWilkins@RitaWilkins.com

Have Rita Wilkins
The Downsizing Designer
Speak at Your Next Conference
or Corporate Retreat

Rita will inspire your audience to reimagine, reinvent, and redesign their lives so they can achieve optimum personal and professional life balance, success and fulfillment.

Rita's engaging and interactive sessions range from a one-hour keynote to a one-day workshop and offer fresh insights into what it takes to design and live a life you love.